roadside geology

of texas

Robert A. Sheldon

MOUNTAIN PRESS PUBLISHING CO.
279 West Front Street
Missoula, Montana 59801

Library of Congress Cataloging in Publication Data

Sheldon, Robert A.
    Roadside geology of Texas.

    Includes bibliographical references.
    1. Geology—Texas—Guide-books. 2. Roads—
Texas. I. Title.
QE167.S53   557.64   79-10950
ISBN 0-87842-103-3 pbk.

MOUNTAIN PRESS PUBLISHING CO.
279 West Front Street
Missoula, Montana 59801

dedication

to Amalie and Arwen

The sea is his, and he made it;
And his hands prepared the dry land.

Psalm 95

preface

Highway travel can be so easy and monotonous as to reach the point of boredom and the danger of drowsiness; this is perhaps a more prevalent condition in Texas with its large expanses of open country and its excellent road network than in most states. A frequently quoted but anonymous remark about Texas describes the State as consisting of "miles and miles of miles and miles."

To even the casually observant driver this need not be the case. Texas is endowed with unusually interesting geology well expressed in its varied land forms, and one need not be a professional geologist to enjoy them. After all, as Alt and Hyndman have so aptly said in Roadside Geology of the Northern Rockies, geology "is the foundation of the scenery because landscape, after all, is geology with trees growing on it."

The geology of Texas has been the subject of extensive study since the first Spanish explorers visited the area in the early 1500's. Scientific literature abounds with regional and detailed geological descriptions; but, necessarily, most of these are couched in such scientific language and presented in such a way as to be of interest and use only to the professional geologist. In this book some of the pertinent parts of this mass of data are summarized in a form and language comprehensible to the layman who has occasion to travel Texas highways by car. The use of scientific jargon is avoided and the roadside geology is described as it can be seen by anyone traveling the highways with only limited time to stop or make side trips. Those travelers with geologic backgrounds and with more penetrating curiosity are referred to the voluminous literature on the subject, a minute part of which is listed in the bibliography.

To give a foundation for understanding Texas geology the first part of this book offers a simplified geological time-table which translates geologic age terms into years. There follows a capsule description of the geological events that have led to the development of the land surfaces seen in driving across the state. Although this part of the book may make heavy reading for the uninitiated, it provides a useful background for the understanding of the road guides that follow, and it is recommended that it be read before using the individual guides.

The preparation of this book has been a pleasure as well as a challenge. I am deeply indebted to a multitude of geologists who have studied and described various aspects of Texas geology and upon whose work I have drawn freely. I am also indebted to many non-geologists whose interest in the landscape and its causes, and whose many penetrating and sometimes embarrassing queries convinced me that such a book should be written. These people are far too numerous to be thanked individually, and I will mention here only the Bureau of Economic Geology of the University of Texas which has been most generous in providing access to reference material, and – through its staff – criticism, comment and encouragement.

contents

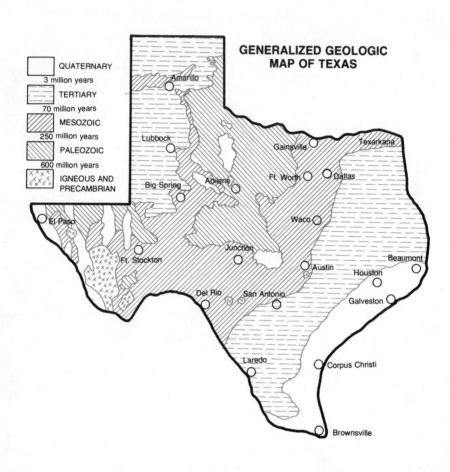

GENERALIZED GEOLOGIC
MAP OF TEXAS

QUATERNARY
3 million years
TERTIARY
70 million years
MESOZOIC
250 million years
PALEOZOIC
600 million years
IGNEOUS AND
PRECAMBRIAN

Amarillo
Lubbock
Gainsville
Texarkana
Ft. Worth
Dallas
Abilene
Big Spring
Waco
El Paso
Ft. Stockton
Junction
Beaumont
Austin
Houston
Del Rio
San Antonio
Galveston
Laredo
Corpus Christi
Brownsville

geologic framework

When the Planet Earth first took form some four billion years ago, molten matter near the surface solidified to become rock, and natural processes which continue to the present day began. Seas formed, rains and winds took their toll of upland areas and moving currents of air and water deposited broken and dissolved rock as sediments. As the first three billion or so years of Earth's history passed, the seas advanced and re-treated to deposit extensive sands, silts and muds which have since been mostly altered by heat, pressure and chemical processes to form various metamorphic rocks of the so-called *Pre-Cambrian* time. Successively throughout *Paleozoic* time, 600 million to 300 million years ago, the seas continued their restless cycles with each depositing its share of sediments. All have left their records in Texas although in some areas there was little marine influence and the sediments were largely transported by winds.

Cambrian and *Ordovician* times 600 million to 500 million years ago, marked the first appearance of animal life as we know it on Earth. The seas were generally shallow and warm, and deposited mostly lime-bearing muds to form limestones that are now one of the principal reservoirs of oil and gas in West Texas. The earliest deposits are the sands and gravels laid down as the seas advanced south-eastward onto the *Pre-Cambrian* landmass.

During *Silurian* and *Devonian* times the seas that covered much of the Central and Western areas were generally quiet, receiving only small amounts of sediment from the lowland areas, and these at a very slow rate. The limy and siliceous rocks of this age contain fossils showing fish as the dominant form of life in the sea, with primitive plants developing on the land.

1

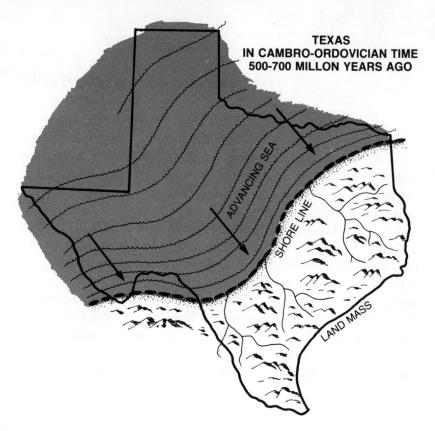

**TEXAS
IN CAMBRO-ORDOVICIAN TIME
500-700 MILLON YEARS AGO**

ADVANCING SEA

SHORE LINE

LAND MASS

Sediments deposited in *Carboniferous* time, when great deposits of coal accumulated, give evidence of a change in conditions that led to the development of large, westward-flowing rivers which deposited great amounts of mud and some sand into the western sea. Deltas similar to that at the present mouth of the Mississippi river formed along what was then the coast; great limestone banks formed off shore. Huge ferns dominated the landscape, and insects and true reptiles first appeared. Much of the oil and gas produced in North Texas originates in rocks of this age.

Rocks of *Permian* age, at the end of the *Paleozoic Era*, show a marked change from earlier conditions. Seas were restricted until only a large inland sea remained in far West Texas. As the seas dried up, the evaporating waters left wide-spread deposits of salt, some of which are mined today near the New

Mexico border. At the same time, great limestone reefs formed, composed of the skeletons of marine animals, similar in nature to the Great Barrier Reef of Australia. The most spectacular exposure of such a reef is at El Capitan, which at 8,751 feet is the highest point in Texas, located in Guadalupe Park in far West Texas.

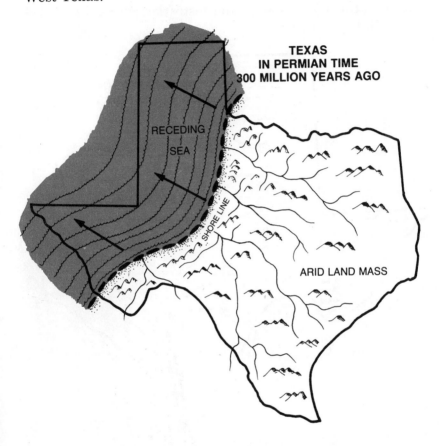

TEXAS
IN PERMIAN TIME
300 MILLION YEARS AGO

RECEDING SEA

SHORE LINE

ARID LAND MASS

At the beginning of *Mesozoic* time, some 250 million years ago, Texas was largely a land area. Only limited lake deposits of *Triassic* and *Jurassic* age exist as clues to its history. However, the nature and distribution of land and sea deposits of this age show a marked reversal on a broad scale of the conditions that generally prevailed during the *Paleozoic* time. The great land-mass which had existed along the present Gulf Coast subsided, and the seas advanced from the east. Most of the rocks in West and Central Texas were deposited by rivers

3

and by the wind. In East Texas and the Gulf Coastal Plain, the seas alternately advanced and retreated, leaving deposits of sand and mud. When the retreat of the sea was obstructed, the waters evaporated and left thick layers of salt. This salt, which behaves as a viscous fluid under higher temperature and pressure, has been squeezed upward to form the salt domes characteristic of this region today. An illustration of this is included in the Gulf Coast section.

TEXAS IN JURASSIC TIME 250 MILLION YEARS AGO

Oscillating Shore Line

Cretacous time, beginning some 180 million years ago, was marked by one of the most wide-spread periods of flooding of the land in geological history. All of Texas was shallowly flooded during part of this time by inland seas in which were deposited great layers of nearly continuous limy muds which now make up the limestone and marl of much of the "Hill

4

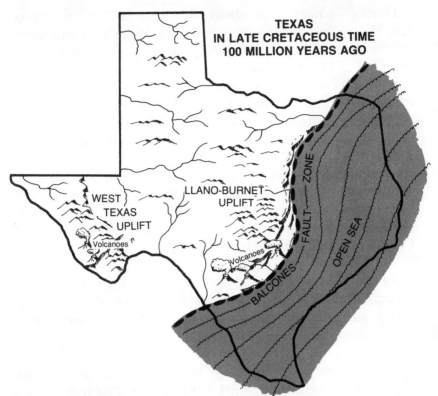

**TEXAS
IN LATE CRETACEOUS TIME
100 MILLION YEARS AGO**

WEST
TEXAS
UPLIFT

Volcanoes

LLANO-BURNET
UPLIFT

Volcanoes

BALCONES FAULT ZONE

OPEN SEA

Country" of Central Texas and vast plains of South West Texas. In and around these seas the huge reptiles or "dinosaurs" that had appeared earlier in primitive form flourished and reached their peak. The ancestral forms of modern life, both animal and plant, made their first appearance toward the end of the *Cretaceous*. It is for good reason that this part of geologic time is called "Mesozoic" or Middle-Life, as it embraces in Earth's history, the transition between the "Paleozoic" or Ancient-Life and the "Cenozoic" or Common, now-known life. The *Cretaceous* also saw the beginning of the deformation of the Earth's crust which is fundamentally responsible for the present-day aspect of Texas. The Llano-Burnet Uplift or the Central Mineral Region of Central Texas began to take its present form, and folding and faulting of the Earth's surface formed high mountains in West Texas. These movements were related to the much greater disturbance of the Earth's crust that formed the Rocky Mountains to the north and west.

During *Tertiary* time, about 80 million to 3 million years ago, the surface of Texas gradually acquired its present form. At the start of *Tertiary* time the eastern shore of what is now the Gulf of Mexico extended along an irregular line roughly from Eagle Pass north-eastward through the Dallas-Ft. Worth area. Later this coast-line gradually receded south-eastward to its present position, depositing layers of sand and mud more than 50,000 feet (15,000 m) thick along the present coast. The great weight of these sediments caused fracture zones, or "faults," forcing some of the underlying salt upward to form salt domes, which penetrated many thousands of feet into the overlying sediments. These movements provided the conditions responsible for many of the oil and gas fields in the Gulf Coast area, and are illustrated in that section.

As the seas withdrew, coastal swamps near river deltas accumulated decayed vegetation which formed the lignite layers, some of which are now being mined as a crude form of coal as shown in the chapter on East Texas.

While the marine sediments of the *Tertiary* were accumulating in the eastern zone, West Texas was a land from which rivers carried sediment to be deposited to the east. This relatively quiet time was interrupted near the end of the Tertiary by volcanic activity in northern Mexico and West Texas. Molten rock penetrated the older sediments, creating extensive sheets of lava and volcanic ash in West Texas. Toward the end of Tertiary time, rivers flowing from the renewed uplift of the Rocky Mountains left extensive flood deposits of gravel, sand, and clay in the High Plains. These deposits form the surface of the vast plains area of the Panhandle which the early Spanish explorers called the "Llano Estacado," or "staked plains" because they found that the only way to retrace their steps across the featureless area was to drive stakes at visible intervals.

The *Tertiary* period ended and the *Quaternary* began with the onset of the ice ages some three million years ago. The great ice sheets of the continental glaciers did not reach Texas, but their effects are readily seen in many areas. As the glaciers advanced, more and more sea water was converted to ice and the general sea-level was correspondingly lowered. As they retreated because of extensive melting, wide-spread flooding by the ancestors of present-day rivers deposited vast sheets of gravel and sand which may be seen wherever the lower *Quaternary* rocks of the *Pleistocene* are exposed.

Although the first primitive tool-using man, *Homo habilis,* is now believed to have appeared on Earth some two million years ago, it was only about 20,000 years ago that he reached Texas on his migration from Asia across the Arctic area and thence southward. Thus, the tenure of man in Texas represents only about one two-hundred-thousandth part of the geologically recorded history of the state. If the history of the Earth were represented by one year, the span of man's life upon its surface would be included within the last hour of time, and that of man in Texas within the last minute. That should give pause to even the most dedicated Texan.

GEOLOGIC TIME CHART

Era	Epoch	Period or Series	Development of Life Forms	Millions of Years	Graphic scale
CENOZOIC	QUATERNARY	Recent	Man		7
		Pleistocene		3	
	TERTIARY	Pliocene	Apes Birds Mammals		25
		Miocene			
		Oligocene			
		Eocene			60
		Paleocene		70	
MESOZOIC	SECONDARY	Cretaceous	Reptiles		
		Jurassic			
		Triassic		250	
PALEOZOIC	PRIMARY	Permian	Land Plants Insects Amphibians		
		Pennsylvanian			
		Mississippian			
		Devonian			
		Silurian	Fishes Marine Plants Shell Fish Scavengers		
		Ordovician			
		Cambrian		600	
ARCHEOZOIC — PROTEROZOIC		Pre-Cambrian	Jelly Fish Corals Algae		
			Bacteria	4,000	

ORIGIN OF THE EARTH

highways

Texas offers the traveler a view of the geologic history of our planet that is perhaps more complete than that to be seen in any other state. Older rocks are known in parts of Minnesota, Greenland, and Africa, but almost every important event since the origin of the earth can be found recorded in the rocks of Texas. The oldest rocks in Texas are in the central part — the so-called Central Mineral Region or Llano-Burnet uplift — and have been radiometrically dated as three billion years old, long before life in any form appeared on Earth.

The purpose of this book is to help the non-geologist read the story in the landscape as he travels across Texas. The geology of the state as a whole is reviewed above. But the geology is so varied it can best be dealt with by dividing the state into seven geologic-geographic regions, as shown on the following map.

The boundaries used for these areas are those generally accepted by various state agencies for non-geological purposes. However, as the topography, soil type, and vegetation that dictate the use of the land are controlled by the geology, this division of the state is also a geological one.

The following pages deal with the state by area. Most road travel through Texas is assumed to be along the Interstate highways. They are described first, followed by the major U.S. highways and a selection of the more travelled State and local routes where often the more interesting geology is to be seen. In many cases the scenically — and thus geologically — most spectacular areas are situated in various national and state parks and monuments. Anyone desiring a more detailed account of these areas is referred to the pertinent publications — some of which are written for non-geologists — as listed in Chapter XII.

The highway key and physiographic diagram shows commonly used local names plus each of the roads covered in this book. The only exceptions are those for certain minor side trips which cannot be accomodated on this scale. Any routes not shown here are included on the more detailed individual maps.

PHYSIOGRAPHIC DIAGRAM
SHOWING
LOCAL AREA NAMES
AND HIGHWAYS COVERED

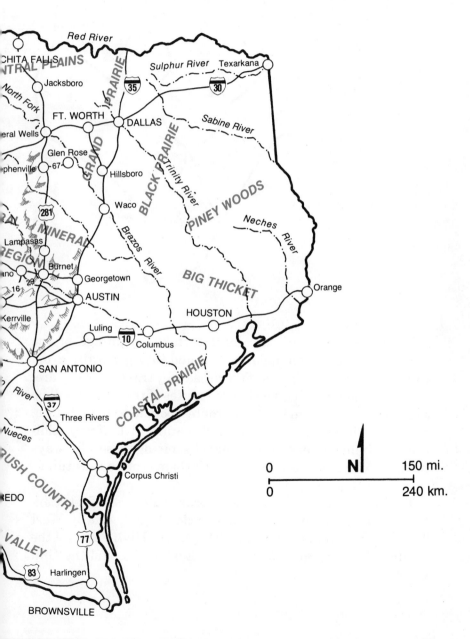

Interstate Highways are built to take advantage of the easiest route between major points, and thus generally avoid the more interesting parts of the areas they traverse. They are, however, the most frequently used routes of travel and will be dealt with first. Often the lesser routes, both federal and state, offer more interesting scenery and require little if any additional driving time. Descriptions of some of these highways have been included, and travel along them is often rewarding.

The area containing the oldest rocks is discussed first. Central Texas holds this honor and is closely followed by West Texas. Then come North Central Texas, the High Plains of the Panhandle area, Southwest Texas, East Texas, and the Gulf Coast.

central texas

Largely because of its harder and more folded rocks and the consequently rougher topography, the heart of Central Texas has been avoided by the interstate highway system. Only I-35 and I-10 enter Central Texas, and these only along the eastern and southern borders of this region. However, Central Texas offers some of the most interesting geology in the state, and is crossed by numerous other highways which provide fascinating opportunities to observe the effects of the diverse geology on the present surface.

The Landsat view gives an outstanding view of much of Central Texas. It was taken by a scanning TV-like technique as part of the remote-sensing coverage of the entire Earth from an unmanned satellite circling at an altitude of 570 miles or 918 kilometers. This particular view was taken in the winter of 1976. It covers an area of approximately 13,000 square miles (34,000 square kilometers) and measures about 115 miles (185 kilometers) on a side. As may be seen on the accompanying explanatory sketch, this constitutes the area from well north of Georgetown to some 50 miles (80 kilometers) east of San Antonio and as far west as Fredericksburg.

The Balcones Fault Zone, curving northeast from San Antonio through Austin and Georgetown and beyond is readily visible because of the striking change in drainage patterns and land forms due to the presence of older and harder folded rocks to the northwest and the younger and more easily eroded rocks to the south and east. Man's effect on the land's surface may be seen in the towns and highways, the limestone quarries which appear as white blotches near Georgetown, New Braunfels, and San Antonio, and the highland lakes formed in the hill country by the damming of the rivers. The construction of these dams was undertaken to control the periodic flooding and to

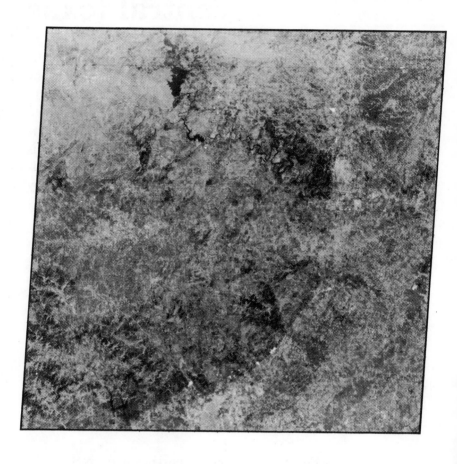

LANDSAT View of Central Texas
Courtesy of Texas Natural Resources Information System, Austin, Texas

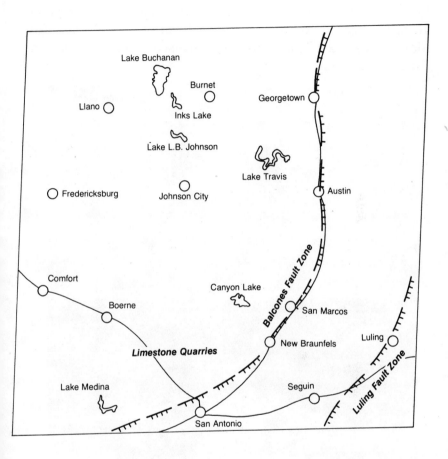

Explanation of Landstat image of Central Texas.

provide water during times of drought, but has paid immense dividends by offering recreational areas for parks, camping, swimming, fishing and boating. A good example of this may be seen in the photo of the lower part of Lake Travis which is formed by the Mansfield Dam across the Colorado River some 15 miles west of Austin via Ranch Road 2222 and Farm-to-Market Road 620. This is the easternmost of the major lakes in the Landsat scene.

Boat harbor or marina on southeast shore of Lake Travis. The entire shoreline is limestne and marl of the Lower Cretaceous Trinity Group.

interstate 10
san antonio — kerrville
— junction

This stretch of highway stays entirely within sedimentary rocks of the Cretaceous. These range from the lower part of the lower Cretaceous to the upper part of the upper Cretaceous, although the latter are seen only near San Antonio. The remainder of the route remains in rocks of the lower Cretaceous. Neither the base nor the top of the Cretaceous System is exposed.

The rocks are primarily limestones and shales deposited in shallow Cretaceous seas as limy ooze and mud from perhaps 180 to 80 million years ago. Other than broad, gentle upward arching which is barely perceptible and is caused by the uplift of the old rocks of the Central Mineral Region just to the north, little has happened to these rocks since they solidified. The strata are essentially horizontal except in the southeastern-most 20 miles (32 kilometers) near San Antonio, where the rock layers are broken and tilted by extensive faulting in the Balcones Fault Zone. Farther northwest, the exposure of rocks of different ages within the lower Cretaceous is due to erosion. Streams have cut down into the older layers, leaving the younger rocks to form the intervening hills.

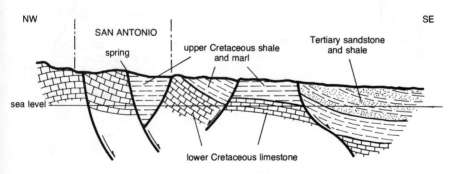

Diagrammatic section of Balcones fault zone at San Antonio.

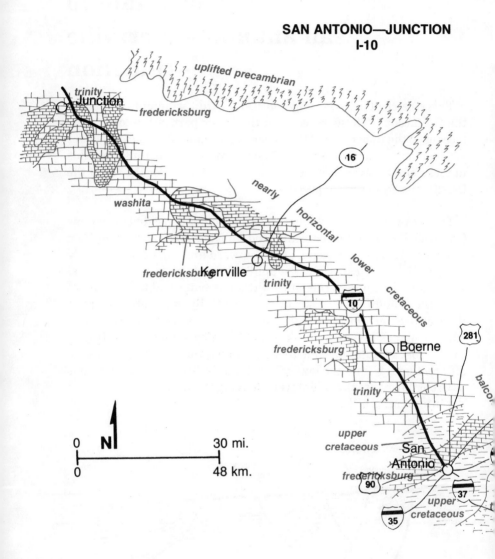

SAN ANTONIO—JUNCTION
I-10

uplifted precambrian

trinity
Junction
fredericksburg

16

nearly

washita

horizontal

fredericksburg Kerrville
trinity
lower
cretaceous

10

281

fredericksburg
Boerne

trinity

balco

upper
cretaceous San
Antonio

fredericksburg
90
37

upper
35 cretaceous

0 ———————— 30 mi.
N
0 ———————— 48 km.

The alternation of hard limestones with softer and more readily eroded shales resulting in the local topographic relief is due to oscillations in sea level. Limestones were deposited in deeper and quieter waters farther from shore.

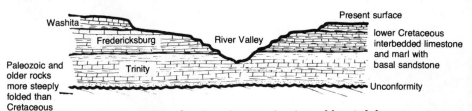

Diagrammatic section showing river erosion into older rock layers.

The lower Cretaceous is divided into three groups, the Trinity, Fredericksburg, and Washita, from bottom to top. That is the sequence in which they were deposited by the warm, quiet sea that covered the area from about 180 million to 100 million years ago.

Between the Balcones Fault Zone and Kerrville, I-10 stays almost entirely on rocks of the oldest or Trinity Group with hills of the Fredericksburg group exposed to the south in the Boerne area, and in a small exposure just east of Kerrville.

Between Kerrville and Junction, the geology and topography are more varied, and almost the entire Lower Cretaceous section is seen. In general the younger groups—the Fredericksburg and the Washita—are preserved on the higher elevations and the Trinity is found in deeper valleys. The best exposures are seen in the vicinity of Junction where the North Llano and South Llano Rivers join to form the Llano River and erosion has been more active. Here the red sandy clays of the basal part of the Trinity Group are exposed.

Looking westward over the Edwards Plateau; its upper surface is limestone of the Fredericksburg Group.

Trinity limestone near Kerrville.

SITES OF GEOLOGIC INTEREST

Limestone Quarries: About 10 miles northeast of the center of San Antonio, the limestones of the Cretacous — both upper and lower — are extensively quarried for building material and the manufacture of cement. The upper Cretaceous limestones are preferred for the latter because of the relative absence of such contaminating elements as silica and iron. But the upper Cretaceous is preserved only where it has been dropped down by the fractures along the Balcones Fault Zone, as shown on the sketch on p. 25.

The extent of these quarrying operations can be appreciated from the fact that they show up as white blotches on the satellite image which was taken from an altitude of 570 miles (920 kilometers). The following photo shows some of these operations as seen from the highway.

Quarry in Cretaceous limestone on Interstate 10 ten miles (16 km.) northwest of San Antonio.

"Stair-step" effect on hillside, caused by alternating hard and soft layers of the lower Cretaceous limestones and marls.

Stair-step Hills: Between Boerne and Kerrville the hillsides have a pronounced "stair-step" aspect, as shown in the photo. This is due to the alternation of hard and soft layers which weather or erode at different rates.

Thin-bedded limestone and marl of the Washita Group shows folds and small faults. Geologists use the term "penecontemporaneous" or "syngenetic" folding.

Contorted Bedding: Along the stretch of I-10 between about 20 miles (32 kilometers) west of Kerrville and the vicinity of Junction, the roadcuts expose a very interesting geological phenomenon. The general attitude of the rock layers is uniform and nearly horizontal, as may be seen in the thicker and more massive limestone beds. However, locally the thinner beds of the softer intervening marl and limestone are contorted into diminutive folds and faults, and give a first appearance of having been buckled by stresses in the Earth.

Close-up of lower Cretaceous. The white layers are solid limestone with hard nodules of chert and flint; the darker layers are softer marl which erodes more easily. The flint was favored by the Indians for arrow points, scrapers and other tools, and fragments or even good artifacts of worked rock are often found in this area.

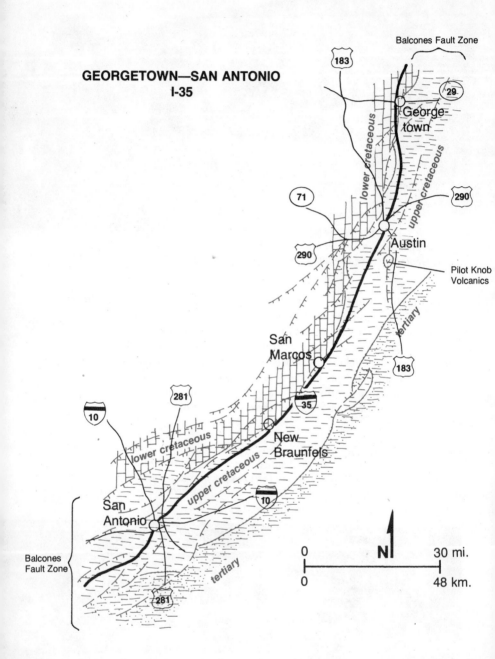

GEORGETOWN—SAN ANTONIO
I-35

Balcones Fault Zone

183

29

George-
town

lower cretaceous

upper cretaceous

71

290

290

Austin

Pilot Knob
Volcanics

tertiary

San
Marcos

183

281

10

lower cretaceous

New
Braunfels

upper cretaceous

10

San
Antonio

281

Balcones
Fault Zone

tertiary

N

0   30 mi.

0   48 km.

interstate 35
georgetown — austin
—san antonio

This entire stretch of I-35 follows the Balcones Fault Zone, crossing and re-crossing the numerous individual faults of which it is composed. These are normal faults, almost always down toward the coast — that is the younger rocks are dropped down on the east side against the older rocks to the west. All the rocks in the area are of Cretaceous age, ranging from the Trinity Group at the base of the lower Cretaceous to the Navarro Group at the top of the upper Cretaceous. They were deposited as limy muds and oozes with rare sands on the sea bottom during the period from about 180 to 80 million years ago.

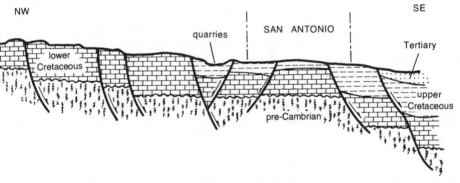

Schematic section through San Antonio along I-10.

The Balcones Fault when seen from a high altitude is a striking topographic feature as may be appreciated from the Landsat image. As seen from the highway level it is less spectacular, but is evident in most areas because the harder rocks to the west form hills rising noticeably above the more deeply eroded, softer and younger rocks to the east. It was this topographic expression that caused the early Spaniards to call it "Los Balcones" or "the balconies." This feature is most evident along I-35 between Austin and New Braunfels where the fault is more pronounced, and the highway stays primarily on the upper Cretaceous rocks on the eastern or down-dropped side.

Large springs are common along the fault zone; most of the fresh water comes from the porous Edwards limestones of the lower Cretaceous which are exposed at the surface in the higher country to the west. Rain water entering the rocks where they are at the surface flows downward and through them until its passage is blocked by the Balcones Fault, where it is forced upward to the surface along the fracture zones. The best known of these springs are at Austin, San Marcos and San Antonio.

The influence that the Balcones Fault Zone with its abundant springs has had on the colonization and development of Texas by Indians, Spaniards and Anglo-Americans is well described on the marker placed by the Texas Historical Commission on Loop 360 just west of Austin.

Limestones of both the lower and the upper Cretaceous are quarried extensively for road and building material and the manufacture of cement. Such quarries and factories may be seen throughout this section of I-35.

SITES OF GEOLOGIC INTEREST

Inner Space Caverns: These caves, along the west side of I-35 one mile south of Georgetown, are interesting, and offer a pleasant cooling respite to the driver as well as a good look at the Lower Cretaceous from the inside. The caves were discovered during the construction of I-35 when the bit on a test drill suddenly dropped into empty space. Like other limestone caverns, they were formed when under-ground water circulating through fractures dissolved the limestone. In this case, the fractures were the result of movement of the rocks along the fault zone.

Pilot Knob: Pilot Knob—a distinctive group of low rounded hills formed of volcanic rocks—is a geological and topographic anomaly in this area of marine sediments. It is shown on the map as a roughly circular area just south of Austin labeled "Pilot Knob Volcanics."

Schematic section across I-35 south of Austin.

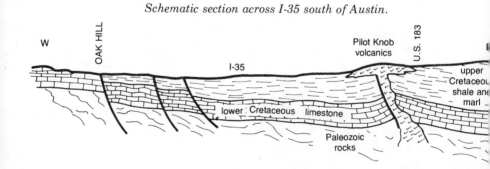

During the later part of the Mesozoic Era when fractures of the earth first occurred along the Balcones Fault Zone, molten igneous rocks welled up from beneath the earth's crust and spread out as a submarine volcano. These molten rocks solidified on the sea bottom and were then covered by limy muds which formed the limestones. These have since eroded away.

To reach this locality, take the Bluff Springs exit, five miles south of Austin and drive eastward about five miles. You will cross the Pilot Knob volcanic rocks before reaching U.S. 183. Watch for signs indicating the route southward to the Cottonmouth School. Along this road you will see brownish-black rocks contrasting sharply with the white limestones and marking where molten rock—in this case, basalts—flowed out on the late Mesozoic sea floor. The rocks are no longer spectacular, but the great columns of steam,when super-heated lava exuded onto the floor of the shallow Mesozoic seas, must have been an awesome sight to the dinosaurs of the time.

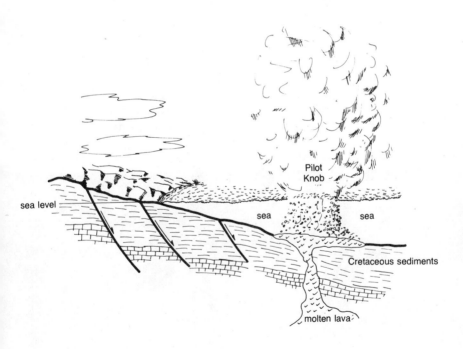

Pilot Knob as it must have appeared in late Cretaceous time some 100 million years ago.

One of the springs which form the San Antonio River is a lily-pad-covered pool.

San Antonio River: One of the attractive features of San Antonio is the San Antonio River which has its source in the springs at the north end of Brackenridge Park. In recent years, wells have been drilled to help control the water flow from these springs. But some of the original flow forming the headwaters of the San Antonio River can still be seen by turning west off Broadway (U.S. 81 Business) on Hildebrand for a halfmile. Some of the springs can be seen within 100 yards of the bridge.

Spring bubbles up to form the San Antonio River.

This is a complex part of the Balcones fault system with many converging and intersecting faults. Some are down-dropped on the northwest, but the overall movement of the Cretaceous rocks along the fault zone is down to the southeast.

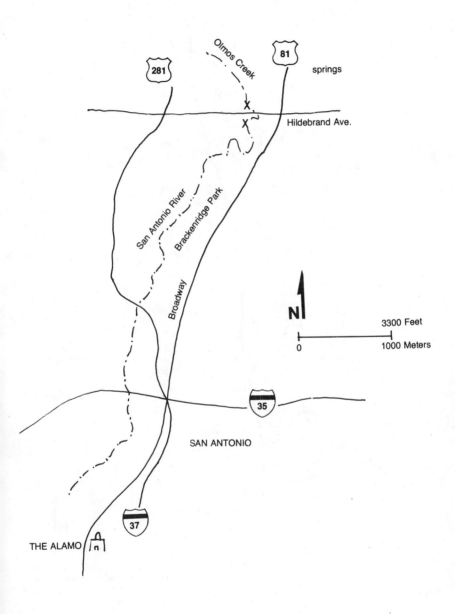

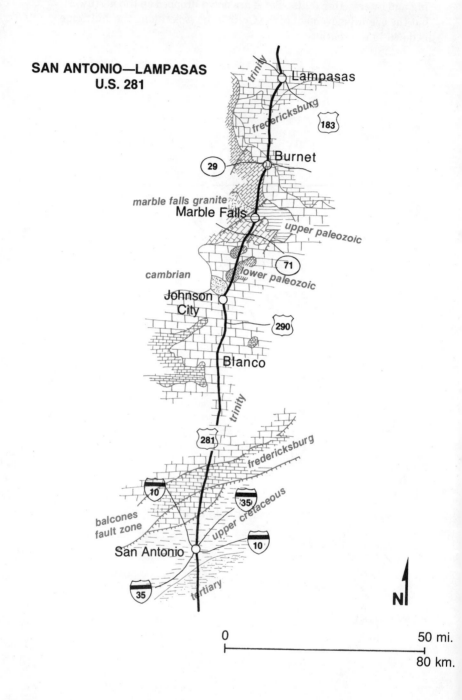

SAN ANTONIO—LAMPASAS
U.S. 281

trinity

Lampasas

fredericksburg

183

29   Burnet

marble falls granite

Marble Falls

upper paleozoic

71

cambrian   lower paleozoic

Johnson
City

290

Blanco

trinity

281

fredericksburg

10

35

balcones
fault zone

upper cretaceous

10

San Antonio

35   tertiary

N

0   50 mi.

80 km.

u.s. 281
san antonio — lampasas

This highway crosses Central Texas from south to north, staying within lower Cretaceous rocks 180 to 100 million years old. The only exceptions are slightly younger upper Cretaceous rocks along the Balcones Fault Zone near San Antonio and the more extensive exposures of Paleozoic rocks up to 600 million years old along the eastern margin of the Llano-Burnet uplift between Johnson City and Burnet. For convenience in description the lower Cretaceous sediments are divided into the Trinity, Fredericksburg, and Washita Groups from bottom to top.

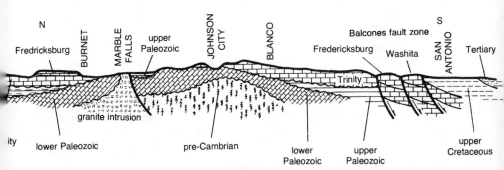

San Antonio to Lampasas along U.S. 281.

Between the Balcones Fault Zone and Johnson City only the Trinity Group is exposed, although just to the south of Johnson City the higher hills to the east and west of the highway are capped by the prominent hard limestone of the Fredericksburg Group. Much of the terrain exhibits the stair-step topography formed by alternating layers of hard, erosion-resistant limestone and more easily eroded layers of marl and shale as described and illustrated in the description of I-10 to the northwest of San Antonio. At Johnson City, the Pedernales River has eroded the rocks almost to the bottom of the Trinity Group, where you can see the reddish-colored sandy sediments that were deposited when the Cretaceous sea first advanced westward over this area deriving its sediments from the much older igneous and metamorphic rocks that then formed the land surface.

Between Johnson City and a point about six miles (10 kilometers) south of Marble Falls, U.S. 281 follows very closely the surface or unconformity which marks the overlap of the Trinity Group onto the Ordovician. The Cretaceous rocks of the Trinity were deposited some 300 million years later than those of the Ordovician, but the present attitude of both is nearly horizontal. This indicates that only minor uplift and depression affected this area for a very long time. Between Round Mountain and the valley of the Pedernales near Marble Falls the higher elevations are in Cretaceous rocks whereas the valleys are eroded down into the Ordovician.

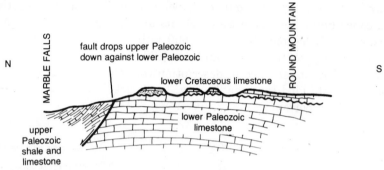

Stream erosion cuts through lower Cretaceous to expose Paleozoic.

The sediments of both ages are predominantly limestones and were deposited at the bottom of similar seas. The rough distinction between the two is made on the more resistant and thicker-bedded character of the Ordovician as opposed to the thinner and more muddy or shaly nature of the Cretaceous. The actual geologic dating is done by a detailed study of the completely different fossil remains of living creatures that inhabited the different seas. These, however, are rarely found in this area.

Between a point five miles south of Marble Falls where Texas 71 crosses U.S. 281, and Burnet, some 20 miles (32 km) to the north, the geology is much more varied. Along this stretch the route crosses the eastern part of the Llano-Burnet uplift and the rocks exposed range in age from the oldest Paleozoic or Cambrian sandstones deposited as much as 600 million years ago to the 140-million-year-old lower Cretaceous limestones.

One mile north of the intersection of Texas 71 and U.S. 281 is an excellent exposure of lower Paleozoic rocks — in this case hard flint-bearing limestones such as those seen sporadically from Johnson City northward. These were deposited in the Ordovician sea some 500 million years ago. They are overlain here by lower Cretaceous limestones deposited more than 300 million years later. During this great gap or unconformity in the geologic history of the area, many thousands of feet of sediments were deposited and later uplifted and eroded away. A part of this record may be seen between here and Marble Falls where limestones and shales of the lower Pennsylvanian were deposited some 300 million years ago. They are preserved because they were dropped down by a fault against Ordovician rocks which normally underlie them.

Roadcut on U.S. 281 two miles (3 km.) south of Marble Falls. Fossil crinoids indicate the upper Paleozoic age of the thin-bedded limestone which is tilted to the northwest. The contrast between this tilting and the nearly horizontal layers of older and younger rocks nearby is due to faulting.

From the highway just north and south of Marble Falls the view westward shows the rounded hills of the pink granite which forms Granite Mountain. This granite is at least one billion years old. It was brought to the surface along a great fault.

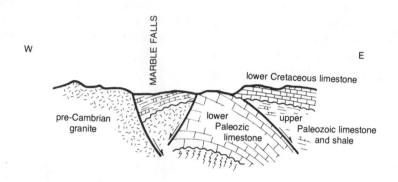

Section at Marble Falls across U.S. 281.

The part of the highway between Marble Falls and Burnet crosses back and forth through rocks of lower and upper Paleozoic age where they are exposed in a complex system of folds and faults. About midway along this route is a quarry in the Ordovician limestone just to the east of the highway. About five miles south of Burnet, Park Road 4 goes westward to the Longhorn Caverns which were formed as lower Paleozoic limestone dissolved in underground water circulating through fractures in the rock.

The skyline to the east between Marble Falls and Burnet is formed by the over-lapping limestones of the lower Cretaceous, and the town of Burnet is built along their contact with the Paleozoic.

Between Burnet and Lampasas, U.S. 281 runs through lower Cretaceous rocks of the Trinity and Fredericksburg Groups. The layers of these rocks are still essentially horizontal and have been altered little since their deposition in lower Cretaceous seas more than 100 million years ago. The hills and valleys record the difference in hardness and thus resistance to erosion of the various layers. Where the softer shaly beds of the Fredericksburg Group are exposed in road cuts many fossil remains of the oysters, clams, and snails which thrived in the limy muds of the shallow seas may be found.

34

Typical lower Cretaceous countryside. The Trinity Group in the valley is overlain by Fredericksburg limestones which form the skyline in the distance.

SITES OF GEOLOGIC INTEREST

Granite Mountain: One mile west of Marble Falls on Farm Road 1431 coarse-grained pink granite is exposed, and one half mile farther a roadside park offers an excellent view of this igneous rock and of the active quarry just south of the highway.

Quarry in Cretaceous limestone on Interstate 10, ten miles (16 Km.) northwest of San Antonio.

Over one billion years ago while this granite was still a red-hot molten liquid, it was forced upward into the older metamorphic rocks deep in the Earth's crust. Thus it cooled very slowly, growing large crystals of quartz and pink feldspar. This is in contrast to the tiny crystals that form in volcanic rocks that are extruded at or near the earth's surface. The eastern margin of this granite mass is marked by a large fault which brings it into contact with much younger Paleozoic sediments; the western margin is the original contact with the metamorphic rocks.

Granite has been quarried here for many years and is widely used for construction; the State capitol in Austin was built of this stone as is the pink granite in part of the Washington Monument in the nation's capitol.

Longhorn Caverns: Fourteen miles (23 kilometers) north of Marble Falls or five miles (8 kilometers) south of Burnet, Park Road 4 runs westward for nine miles (15 kilometers) to the Longhorn Caverns State Park. These caves are the result of the dissolving action of underground waters circulating through fractures in the same lower Paleozoic limestones as those exposed along U.S. 281. They have an interesting history of use by the early Indians and by the first Anglo-American settlers. During the Civil War, gunpowder was stored and possibly manufactured here. The main entrance to the caverns as now used was formed by the collapse of the cave roof into an underground room.

For more information on connecting roads, see;

Chapter IV
    Interstate 10:—San Antonio—Kerrville—Junction
    Interstate 35: Georgetown—Austin—San Antonio
    U.S. 290: Austin—Fredericksburg—Junction
    Texas 29, U.S. 87: Brady—Georgetown
    Texas 71: Austin—Llano

Chapter VI
    U.S. 281: Lampasas—Stephenville
Chapter VIII
    Interstate 35: San Antonio—Laredo
Chapter X:
    Interstate 10: Orange—Houston—San Antonio
    Interstate 37: Corpus Christi—Brownsville

u.s. 290
austin—fredericksburg
—junction

This direct highway west of Austin stays entirely within sediments of Cretaceous age, and affords an excellent view of rocks deposited in early Cretaceous time. The extreme eastern end, on the southern outskirts of Austin, is built on upper Cretaceous clays and marls which were deposited in a muddy sea about 100 million years ago. Within ten miles of I-35 the route crosses the Balcones Fault Zone where the rocks have been broken and those to the west uplifted by 1000 feet (300 meters) or more. This brings the limestones of the oldest part of the Cretaceous — the Trinity Group — to the surface where they form much more rugged hills than the softer rocks of the upper Cretaceous. Between here and Junction, U.S. 290 stays in rocks of the Trinity, Fredericksburg and Washita Groups of the lower Cretaceous. These were deposited on the bottom of the warm quiet sea which covered this part of Texas from about 180 to 100 million years ago. There is some minor faulting, but in a regional sense, the rocks have been raised by the Llano-Burnet uplift into a broad arch which is so gentle as to be barely perceptible.

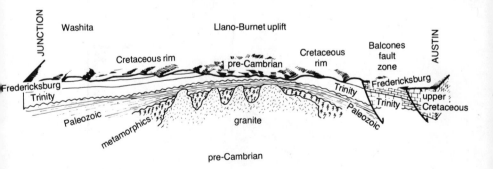

Diagrammatic section from Austin to Junction along U.S. 290.

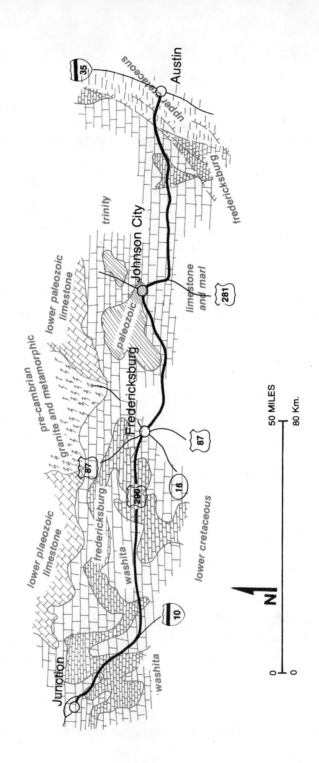

AUSTIN—JUNCTION
U.S. 290

Junction

Austin

35

Johnson City

Fredericksburg

281

87

87

16

290

10

trinity

lower paleozoic limestone

pre-cambrian granite and metamorphic

lower paleozoic limestone

paleozoic

limestone and marl

fredericksburg

washita

lower cretaceous

washita

fredericksburg

upper cretaceous

N

0   50 MILES
0   80 Km.

In general the younger rocks form the higher elevations, with intervening streams eroding downward to expose rocks of the older groups. The entire section is predominantly limestone, but the interlayered shales and marls, which are much more readily eroded away by running water, provide diversified form to the hills and valleys. The marly limestones of the lower part of the Fredericksburg Group are particularly rich in fossil oysters, clams, and snails. These are easily found where this part of the section is exposed.

The harder limestones form flat-topped hills, pronounced ridges along the slopes, and steep-walled bluffs and stream banks.

Between Johnson City and Fredericksburg, where it passes Lyndon B. Johnson State Park, U.S. 290 follows just south of the contact between the Paleozoic sediments deposited some 600 to 400 million years ago and the overlapping lower Cretaceous. This unconformity represents an age gap of several 100 million years, during a good part of which Paleozoic rocks were being eroded prior to the advance of the Cretaceous sea. These softer older rocks, though uplifted by several thousand feet, have been eroded down to form a general topographic low which is encircled by the younger rocks which form a higher and more rugged landscape.

Fossil oysters in marl of the Fredericksburg Group.

For more information on connecting roads, see

texas 16
llano — kerrville

Between Llano and Kerrville, Texas 16 crosses the boundary between the billion or more years old pre-Cambrian granites and metamorphic rocks of the heart of the Llano-Burnet uplift and the rimming lower Cretaceous limestones and marls. These sediments were deposited by shallow seas invading the area from the east and south less than 200 million years ago.

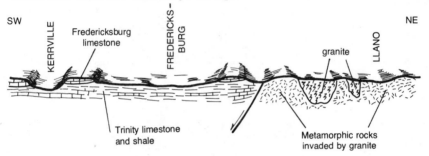

SW · NE · KERRVILLE · Fredericksburg limestone · FREDERICKSBURG · granite · LLANO · Trinity limestone and shale · Metamorphic rocks invaded by granite

Schematic section along Texas 16.

The town of Llano sits in the valley of the eastward-flowing Llano River. It is surrounded by rolling hills made up of the typical coarse, pink granite of Central Texas, and the older metamorphic rocks it intruded more than a billion years ago. These metamorphic rocks were originally deposited as sands and muds as much as three billion years ago and have been metamorphosed by intense heat and pres-

Banded Precambrian gneiss 10 miles (16 km.) south of Llano.

41

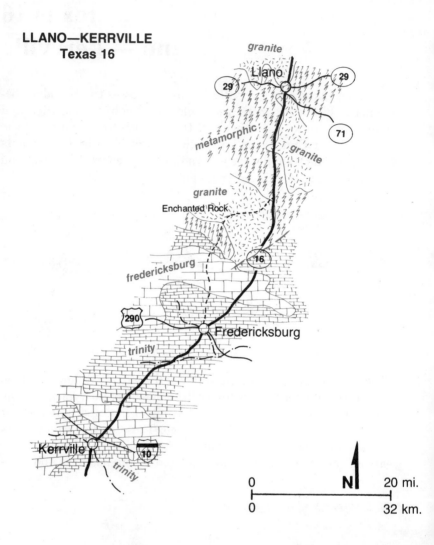

LLANO—KERRVILLE
Texas 16

granite

Llano

29 · 29

71

metamorphic

granite

granite

Enchanted Rock

16

fredericksburg

290

Fredericksburg

trinity

Kerrville

10

trinity

0   N   20 mi.
0   32 km.

Enchanted Rock, as seen from Ranch Road 965.

sure into schists and gneisses. The schists are full of parallel sheets of mica and retain a sedimentary appearance; the gneisses are so altered and recrystallized that they suggest layered granites.

South of Llano, the granite hills can be seen just east of Texas 16, and 12 miles (19 kilometers) south of Llano the highway crosses a small spur of pink granite that juts westward into the metamorphic rocks. Sixteen miles (26 kilometers) south of Llano, Ranch Road 965 branches southwest off Texas 16 and provides an alternate route to Fredericksburg via the Enchanted Rock — a mile-square stock of pink granite described at the end of this section. This great bald rock was sacred to the Indians who fought to preserve it from the white men. It is now a favored spot for hikers, campers and hang-gliders and has been purchased by the state.

Between this point and Fredericksburg to the south, Texas 16 continues in pink to gray granite; the metamorphic rocks are exposed just to the east. After eight miles (13 kilometers) of this, it abruptly enters the white limestone and marl of the Trinity Group of the lower Cretaceous system. This sudden change occurs 14 miles (23 kilometers) north of Fredericksburg at a large fault which dropped the Cretaceous Trinity limestone down into contact with the granite. It is marked by an obvious change in vegetation; the prevailing oaks favor the soil derived from the granite and the scrub cedar or juniper favors the lower Cretaceous rocks.

The town of Fredericksburg is on the Trinity Group where erosion by the Pedernales River has exposed it. The higher hills which are crossed some 10 miles (16 kilometers) north of Fredericksburg and which make up most of the skyline in the area, are composed of the bedded limestones of the overlying Fredericksburg Group which takes its name from this old German-settled town.

South of the broad valley floor of gravel, sand and clay deposited by the Pedernales River, Texas 16 cuts through the Trinity Group in the valley here, and near the Guadalupe River at Kerrville. It cuts through the Fredericksburg Group across the intervening hills.

In the northern outskirts of Kerrville, Texas 16 intersects Interstate 10 before continuing its rather tortuous route between Kerrville and San Antonio by way of Bandera. This last stretch is scenically rewarding but time consuming; and geologically it closely duplicates the lower Cretaceous seen along the faster and more direct Interstate 10.

Spalling of the granite of Enchanted Rock.

SITES OF GEOLOGIC INTEREST

Enchanted Rock: The short side-trip along Ranch Road 965 from Texas 16 between Llano and Fredericksburg offers an unusual view of a large granite batholith. The magma or molten rock intruded upward into the older solid rocks and solidified and crystallized slowly at a great depth below the surface. This allowed large crystals to develop, and in this area those of quartz and pink feldspar are often an inch (2 or 3 centimeters) across.

The rounded form is due to the concentric manner in which the granite spalls, or peels off, in onion-like layers caused by alternate contraction and expansion with temperature changes. This peeling-off of great angular slabs of rock can be seen from the entrance to the park and camp ground just off Ranch Road 965 about eight miles (13 kilometers) from Texas 16.

For more information on connecting roads, see Chapter IV.

Interstate 10: San Antonio—Kerville—Junction
U.S. 290: Austin—Fredericksburg—Junction
Texas 29, U.S. 87: Brandy—Georgetown
Texas 71: Austin—Llano

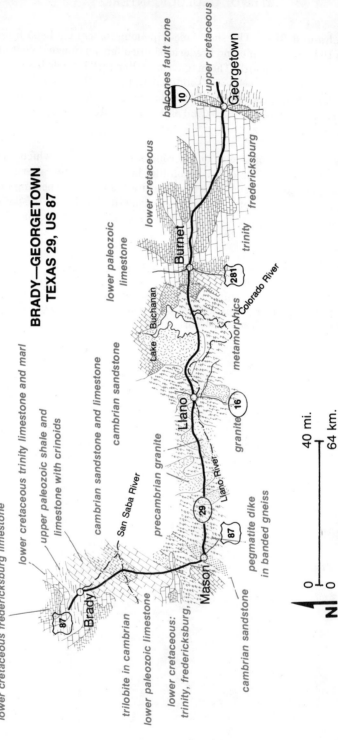

**BRADY—GEORGETOWN
TEXAS 29, US 87**

lower cretaceous fredericksburg limestone

lower cretaceous trinity limestone and marl

upper paleozoic shale and
limestone with crinoids

cambrian sandstone and limestone

cambrian sandstone

lower paleozoic
limestone

balcones fault zone

upper cretaceous

Georgetown

lower cretaceous

fredericksburg

trinity

Burnet

Colorado River

Lake Buchanan

metamorphics

Llano

granite

Llano River

San Saba River

precambrian granite

Brady

trilobite in cambrian

lower paleozoic limestone

lower cretaceous:
trinity, fredericksburg,

Mason

cambrian sandstone

pegmatite dike
in banded gneiss

0   40 mi.
0   64 km.

N

46

texas 29, u.s. 87
brady — georgetown

This route offers perhaps the best view of the geological history of Central Texas by combining modern highways with good exposures of rocks ranging in age from over three billion years to less than 100 million years. For a traveller crossing Texas from west to east or returning from a visit to West Texas, it provides a welcome relief from the somewhat faster but undeniably more monotonous travel along the Interstate system without any serious sacrifices of travel time.

At Brady, U.S. 87 leaves the valley of Brady Creek which has been eroded down through lower Cretaceous into upper Paleozoic rocks. This unconformable contact, typical of that seen wherever the Llano-Burnet uplift is approached, provides a view of nearly horizontal Cretaceous limestone deposited some 150 million years ago resting upon more steeply dipping Paleozoic shales deposited 150 million years earlier. The shales were tilted and eroded to a fairly flat surface before incursion of the Cretaceous sea.

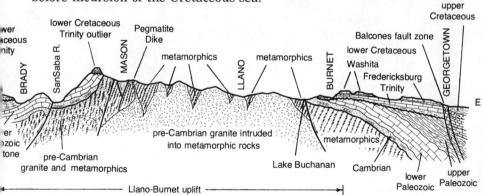

Cross section from Brady to Georgetown.

In road cuts within two miles (3 kilometers) southeast of Brady, hard white limestones which have been fractured and partly recrystallized yield fossil remains of crinoids — marine animals related to modern starfish — of early upper Paleozoic age. These limestones with their associated shales overlie the more massive limestones of the lower Paleozoic, some 200 million years older. They are exposed sporadically almost to the crossing of the San Saba River about 10 miles (16 kilometers) from Brady. Here a fault related to the Llano-Burnet uplift has brought earliest Paleozoic sediments — red sandstones and interbedded algal limestones of the 500-600 million years-old Cambrian Period into contact with the younger rocks.

View downstream along the San Saba River from the U.S. 87 bridge just south of Brady. The river has cut down into Lower Paleozoic limestone.

Four miles (6 kilometers) south of the San Saba River, the rugged nature of the country changes to one of smoothly rounded hills formed by the fine-grained, dark reddish brown sandstones of the Cambrian. Upon exposure to the weather, these sands become dark to bright red due to the oxidation of their iron content. The nearly spherical nature of the quartz grains suggests that they were transported a long distance before being deposited.

48

Six miles (10 kilometers) farther south, or nine miles (15 kilometers) from Mason, U.S. 87 crosses from the Paleozoic sediments into a complex of coarse-grained pink granite intruded in Precambrian time into the older metamorphic rocks. These erode to form the rocky but rounded surface typical of such unstratified rocks.

Rocky but rounded surface formed by granite and gneiss nine miles (15 km.) north of Mason.

Seven miles (11 kilometers) north of Mason, the crest of a prominent ridge crossed by the highway is formed by an outlier or erosional remnant of the lower Cretaceous limestone. It once covered all of this area but has since been almost entirely removed by erosion. From here, the town of Mason, some 300 feet (92 meters) below, can be seen in its Cambrian and older valley rimmed to the south and west by flat-topped Cretaceous hills.

Looking southward from Texas 29 between Mason and Llano. Foreground is Precambrian metamorphic and igneous rocks; skyline is the Lower Cretaceous rim of the uplift.

Typical rounded granite hill just west of Lake Buchanan.

From the court house square in Mason, Texas 29 runs generally eastward for 64 miles (103 kilometers) through Llano to Burnet and thus through the heart of the Llano-Burnet uplift. This entire portion of the highway is built on Precambrian metamorphic and igneous rocks from one to three billion years old. The topography is smoothly rounded with harder and more erosion-resistant granite forming the higher elevations. From the hilltops the extent of this ancient complex of rocks to the south and north can be appreciated; the skyline to the south is dominated by the rim of lower Cretaceous sediments overlapping with a shingle effect onto the older rocks. The lower Cretaceous seas covered the entire area some 150 to 100 million years ago, but their sediments have long since been eroded away from the central part because of its continuing vertical uplift.

The cross sections illustrate the manner in which the Llano-Burnet uplift has developed since the flat eroded surface of the billion or more years old rocks was intermittently covered by the Paleozoic seas from about 600 to 300 million years ago.

At Llano, Texas 29 reaches the Llano River and follows it downstream through the pre-Cambrian metamorphic and granitic rocks until it reaches the point where the Colorado River is dammed to form Lake Buchanan.

The Buchanan Dam as seen from the Texas 29 bridge across the Colorado River at the head of Inks Lake.

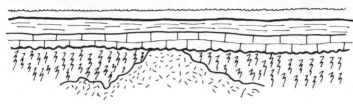

sea level
land surface
upper Paleozoic
lower Paleozoic

pre-Camrian

Upper Paleozoic — 300 million years ago.

land surface

Lower Mesozoic — 200 million years ago.

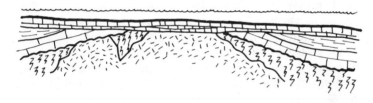

sea level

land surface

Cretaceous

Cretaceous (upper Mesozoic) — 100 million years ago.

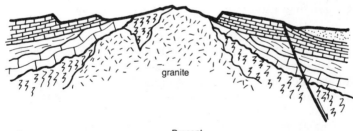

granite

Tertiary

Cretaceous

upper Paleozoic

lower Paleozoic

pre-cambrian

Present.

Development of Llano-Burnet uplift.

51

Packsaddle Mountain, a remnant of Cambrian sandstone resting uncomformably on metamorphics.

The most prominent hills south of Texas 29 near Lake Buchanan include Packsaddle Mountain where the relatively horizontal sandstones of the Cambrian are preserved on top of the strongly folded metamorphic and igneous rocks of the Precambrian.

Lake Buchanan is the largest of the Highland Lakes which are formed by a series of dams built across the Colorado River for flood control, water conservation and electric power generation. As are the other similar lakes, it is a popular center for water sports.

East of Buchanan Dam, Texas 29 runs near the north side of Inks Lake, formed by the next dam below on the Colorado River. After traversing Precambrian rocks to a point approximately midway between Buchanan Dam and the town of Burnet, the highway crosses a fault which has dropped the lower Paleozoic sandstones and limestones down against the older rocks. Just west of Burnet these old sediments are overlain by the lower Cretaceous limestones of the Trinity Group marking the eastern limit of the Llano-Burnet uplift and the start of the unconformable overlap by Cretaceous rocks. As elsewhere around the rim of the uplift, this unconformity represents a geologic gap or hiatus of nearly one half-billion years.

Immediately west of Burnet, Texas 29 climbs the rimming escarpment through the Trinity into the overlying Fredericksburg Group of the lower Cretaceous. For the 34 miles (55 kilometers) between here and the outskirts of Georgetown, the highway is built on limestones and marls of the Fredericksburg Group with the exception of short stretches where erosion has cut through these rocks to expose the upper part of the underlying Trinity Group. At the western limits of Georgetown, the faulting of the Balcones Zone has dropped down and preserved successively younger rocks. In the western part of Georgetown, rocks of the Washita Group which forms the top of the lower Cretaceous system are exposed, and to the east of Interstate 35 the fertile plains of the marls and shales of the upper Cretaceous begin.

Algal Limestone: Just downstream from the bridge where U.S. 87 crosses the San Saba River 10 miles (16 kilometers) south of Brady, the bed of that river is on hard limestone which was deposited in the earliest Paleozoic sea to invade Texas in Cambrian time, some 600 million years ago. This limestone contains excellent fossil remains of algae, an ancestral sea-weed that was one of the first still-recognizable forms of life to develop on Earth. Older specimens of algae are found in Precambrian sediments elsewhere. These lily pad-like fossils make a few minute's visit to the rest area just below the bridge worthwhile.

Cambrian algae in the San Saba River. The individual fossils are about two feet (60 cm.) across.

Pegmatite dike cutting obliquely through banded gneiss east of Mason. The width of the pegmatite is about 2 feet (60 cm).

Pegmatite Dike: When the molten granitic rock was intruded into the older metamorphic rocks in Central Texas a billion or so years ago, some of the rock, dissolved in a gaseous fluid, found its way into fractures and solidified to form the very coarsely-crystalline rock known as pegmatite. The crystals of such rocks, in common with granite, are mostly quartz and feldspar, with mica and other related minerals, and may reach several feet across. A small pegmatite dike or vein of this type is exposed in a road cut on Texas 29 just three miles (5 kilometers) east of Mason.

For more information on connecting roads, see

Chapter IV
  Interstate 35: Georgetown—Austin—San Antonio
  U.S. 281: San Antonio—Lampasas
  Texas 16: Llano—Kerrville
  Texas 71: Austin—Llano
Chapter VI
  U.S. 87: Big Spring—San Angelo—Brady
Chapter IX
  Interstate 35: Georgetown—Dallas

texas 71
austin—llano

This is a very rewarding highway from a geological point of view as it reaches the heart of the Llano-Burnet uplift, and affords a view of geologic events spanning more than one billion years of Earth's history. At Austin the highway is on rocks of upper Cretaceous age which were deposited some 100 million years ago. Westward it crosses the Balcones Fault Zone into lower Cretaceous rocks about 150 million years old, then successively into the upper Paleozoic some 300 million years old, the lower Paleozoic, about 500 million years old and the Precambrian with an age of over one billion years. Although there is much folding and faulting of the rocks to complicate the picture, the geology is rather simple, as shown in the schematic cross-section.

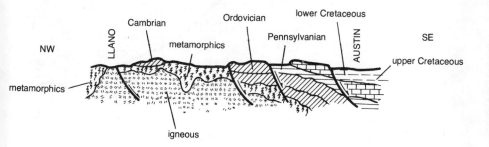

Cross section from Austin to Llano.

The Balcones Fault Zone is a major feature in the geology of Texas. The main trace of this fault zone is crossed at Oak Hill, about seven miles (11 kilometers) from Austin, where the highway encounters lower Cretaceous limestones which provide a marked change in the character of the land, with rough rocky hills replacing the more gentle slopes to the east. About 30 miles (48 kilometers) from Austin, where the road to Spicewood turns off to the north, a change from the rough limestone country to a broad gentle valley marks the overlap of the lower Cretaceous onto black limestones and dark shales of the upper Paleozoic Pennsylvanian System. This unconformable contact

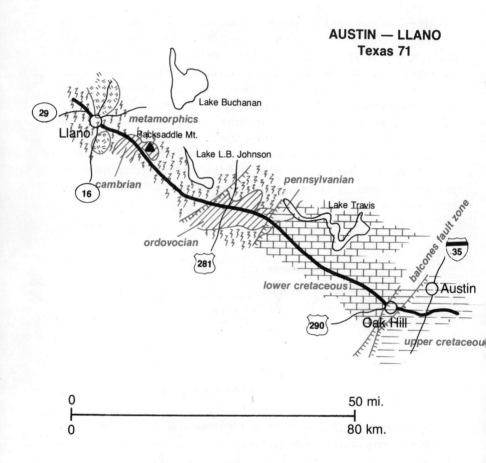

AUSTIN — LLANO
Texas 71

Lake Buchanan

metamorphics

Llano

Packsaddle Mt.

Lake L.B. Johnson

pennsylvanian

Lake Travis

cambrian

ordovocian

balcones fault zone

Austin

lower cretaceous

Oak Hill

upper cretaceous

29

16

281

35

290

```
0                              50 mi.
├──────────────────────────────┤
0                              80 km.
```

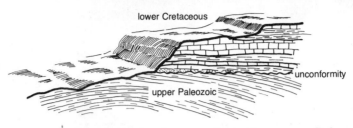

lower Cretaceous

unconformity

upper Paleozoic

Lower Cretaceous sediments overlapping unconformably on upper Paleozoic rocks.

represents a gap in geologic history of some 150 million years during which the area was subjected to erosion before the advance westward of the Cretaceous sea.

View northwestward across the Llano-Burnet uplift from Texas 71 about 30 miles (48 km.) west of Austin. Foreground and skyline are lower Cretaceous; low middleground is Paleozoic and older.

About 40 miles (64 kilometers) from Austin and about three miles (5 kilometers) east of the intersection with U.S. 281, Texas 71 crosses a major fault which brings lower Paleozoic rocks to the surface in contact with the Upper Paleozoic. The older rocks are very hard, light-grey limestones with chert nodules and were deposited by the widespread Ordovician sea about 500 million years ago. The highway continues on Ordovician limestones for about seven miles where a fault brings the Precambrian metamorphic rocks to the surface. These metamorphic rocks were originally deposited as sediments from one to three billion years ago when the Earth was in its primordial stage and the first continents and oceans had been formed. Since that time they have been intruded by igneous rocks and subjected to such intense heat and pressure that they have been completely changed in form — metamorphosed — and have been folded into practically undecipherable convolutions.

Pedernales River cutting through Lower Cretaceous limestone just above Lake Travis.

Between here and Llano, Texas 71 remains on the metamorphic rocks except for a few higher elevations where the red iron-bearing sandstones of the Cambrian are preserved. These sands, the earliest deposits of the Paleozoic, were laid down by wind and water some 600 million years ago. In spite of their extreme age they have been tilted only slightly, which attests to the freedom of this area from any tectonic movement, other than essentially vertical uplift since earliest Paleozoic times.

Packsaddle Mountain: Looking northward from Texas 71 about ten miles (16 km.) southeast of Llano. Foreground is intensely folded Precambrian metamorphics; crest is relatively flat Cambrian sandstone.

Just before entering Llano, the highway crosses exposures of coarse-grained pink granite of pre-Cambrian age. The pink feldspar and white quartz crystals making up the granite occur in crystals of up to one inch (2 or 3 centimeters) across, which reflects their slow cooling at a great depth below the surface.

Lower Paleozoic (Ordovician) limestone near the intersection of Texas 71 and U.S. 281.

For more information on connecting roads, see:

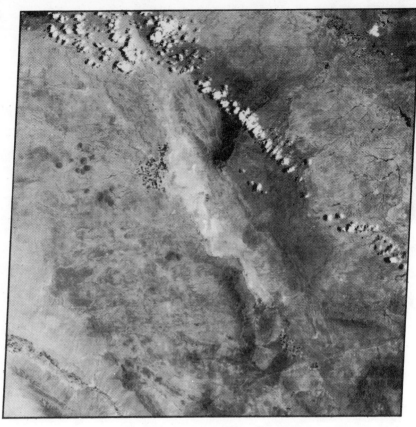

LANDSAT view of West Texas.
Courtesy of Texas Natural Resources Information System Austin Texas

west texas

West Texas, or roughly that part of the state which lies west of the Pecos River, is a geologist's paradise. Its aridity and scarcity of vegetation do not appeal to people who prefer their geology with trees growing on it. But the general lack of vegetation, and therefore of soil cover, gives a rarely equalled view of the geological make-up of the country-side.

The Landsat image (page 14) shows some 13,000 square

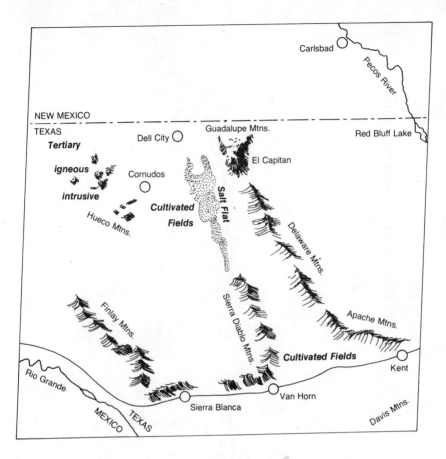

Explanation of Landstat Image of West Texas.

miles (34,000 square kilometers) extending from the Rio Grande in the southwest to New Mexico in the north and the Pecos River in the northeast. Significant tree growth is limited to the valleys of the Rio Grande and the Pecos, and to the higher slopes of the mountain ranges, but neither this nor the sparse brush on the low-lands obscures an overall view of the geology. The principal evidences of man's occupation are in the white trace of Interstate 10 in the southeast and U.S. 180 near the Guadalupe Mountains, the man-made Red Bluff Lake on the Pecos River and the dark splotches of cultivated fields of feed along the major rivers and near Salt Flat and Van Horn.

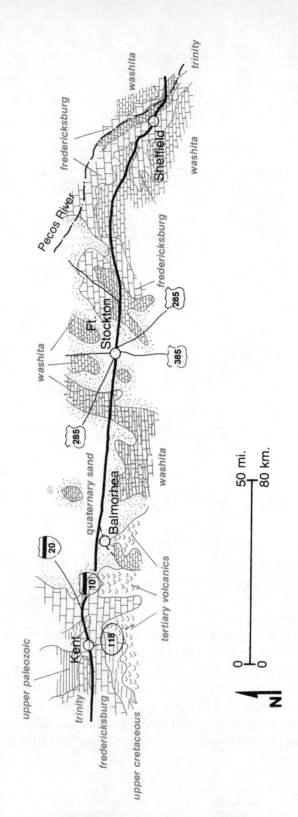

SHEFFIELD—FT. STOCKTON—KENT
I-10

upper paleozoic

trinity

fredericksburg

upper cretaceous

tertiary volcanics

quaternary sand

washita

fredericksburg

washita

trinity

washita

fredericksburg

Pecos River

Kent

Balmorhea

Ft. Stockton

Sheffield

20

10

118

285

385

285

50 mi.

80 km.

N

62

interstate 10
sheffield — ft. stockton
— kent

Sheffield is near the contact of the lower Cretaceous Fredericks-burg Group with the underlying Trinity Group which is exposed in the lowermost slopes of the Pecos River Valley. Fifteen miles (24 kilometers) to the west of Sheffield, I-10, or the old U.S. 290 which it replaces, climbs slowly into the overlying Washita group, the

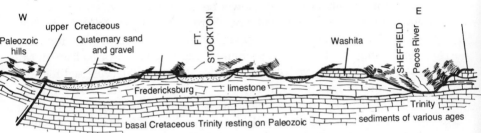

Cross section from Sheffield to Ft. Stockton to Kent along the line of I-10.

youngest of the lower Cretaceous marine sediments. The principal rocks of the lower Cretaceous System throughout much of the entire section of highway are light-colored limestones and marls deposited while the ocean covered this entire area from 160 to 70 million years ago.

Looking southeastward from near Sheffield along I-10 (U.S. 290) across the Pecos Valley. The Pecos River has eroded down into the Trinity Group. The main slopes of the valley walls are Fredericksburg Group and the crest is Washita. The attitude of the rock layers, undisturbed and thus still nearly horizontal after 100 million years, can clearly be seen.

Hills 15 miles (24 km.) west of Sheffield are composed of Fredericksburg limestone and marl capped by flat layers of Washita limestone which have resisted erosion.

The rest of the route to within 15 miles (24 kilometers) of Ft. Stockton remains within the lower beds of the Washita Group except for a short stretch about midway where erosion has cut down into the top of the Fredericksburg Group and allowed deposition of a tongue of very young Quaternary sands blanketing much of the area from here to Kent. Pumping wells that produce oil from Paleozoic sediments thousands of feet below are commonly seen along this stretch, and hills capped by flat-lying limestone of the Washita Group are visible throughout. One of these hills with a distinctive form is a landmark indicating that Ft. Stockton is only a 30-minute drive to the west.

For the last ten miles (16 kilometers) east of Ft. Stockton, I-10 runs on the surface of sands, muds and gravels deposited by periodic flooding within the last hundred thousand years.

I-10 is built on the surface of these same young flood deposits for 50 miles (80 kilometers) west to where the highway crosses the Valley-Southern railway just north of Balmorhea. This deposit is only a thin veneer, frequently interrupted in small areas where the lower Cretaceous Washita limestone is exposed or where its proximity to the surface is indicated by patches of white caliche, which are lime deposits left by evaporation of water which has reached the surface from underlying limestone. The flat-topped hills north and south of the highway are Washita limestone except for a range of darker hills visible some 10 miles (16 kilometers) to the south. These hills mark the limit of the Tertiary volcanic lavas that make up the Davis Mountains. Occasional oil fields produce from upper Paleozoic rocks a few thousand feet below the surface.

Just west of the railroad crossing, I-10 skirts the northern edge of these volcanic rocks where they rest unconformably on the lower Cretaceous. The low rounded hills along the highway are gravels composed primarily of fragments of volcanic rock washed down as alluvial fans from the mountains to the south. Where Cretaceous rocks are exposed, the eastward tilt of the layers gives evidence of the approach to an area of uplift and faulting forming the Apache Mountains north of Kent. Fissures accompanying uplift provided access through which the molten lava reached the surface as a series of volcanic vents to form the Davis Mountains. This folding and faulting affected both upper and lower Cretaceous rocks, and took place during Tertiary time from about 50 to 15 million years ago.

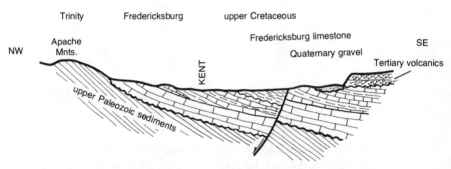

Schematic section across Kent area.

West of the junction with I-20, and 8 miles (15 kilometers) east of Kent, a block of tan marls of upper Cretaceous age has been faulted down and preserved from the erosion which removed the Washita sediments from this area during the time of uplift. Small veins of the variety of gypsum known as selenite occur in a road cut here, and beautiful crystals resembling hoar-frost are easily found.

Kent is situated on lower Cretaceous rocks — limestone and marl — but just north of town the southeastern tip of the Apache Mountains is made up of upper Paleozoic limestone which was deposited some 200 million years before the incursion of the lower Cretaceous sea.

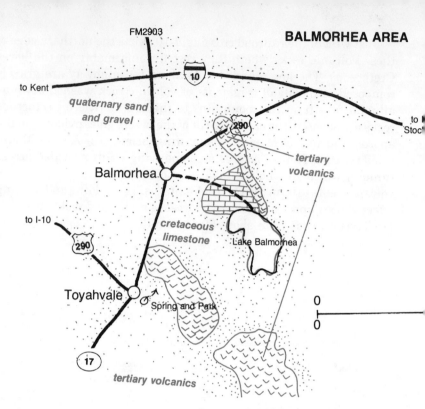

Sketch map of Balmorhea area.

SITES OF GEOLOGIC INTEREST

Balmorhea Springs: A short side trip south of I-10, 20 miles (32 kilometers) east of the junction with I-20, offers a close view of the Tertiary volcanic rocks and the fresh water springs which make the Balmorhea-Toyahvale area an oasis in this arid country. Balmorhea may be reached by turning southward off I-10 on either Farm to Market Road 2903 or old U.S. 290 — a distance of about 3 miles (5 kilometers).

Between I-10 and Balmorhea, U.S. 290 crosses a spur of the Tertiary volcanic rocks which here are a finely crystalline dark grey basalt which because of its iron content weathers to a dark reddish brown. These same basalts rest on the lower Cretaceous limestone at Balmorhea Lake 2 miles (3 kilometers) southeast of that town.

Lake Balmorhea is fed by springs located four miles (6 kilometers) to the south near Toyahvale on Texas 17. Here Texas maintains the Balmorhea State Park which includes the main or San Solomon Spring. It was originally called "Mescalero Spring" because the Mescalero Apaches used its water to grow corn and peaches.

Lake Balmorhea. The foreground is Lower Cretaceous limestone; the background is Tertiary lava.

Before flowing through a diversion channel to Lake Balmorhea, this spring feeds what is touted as "the largest completely spring-fed swimming pool in the world." The pool is drained during the winter season but during the summer is an extremely popular spot.

The waters issue from the Quaternary gravels and sands where they overlie an impervious layer in the basalt. The hills in the background are made of the Tertiary lava flow.

For more information on connecting roads, see

Hill of light colored Lower Cretaceous rocks capped by a remnant of a basalt lava flow erupted in the Tetiary Period.

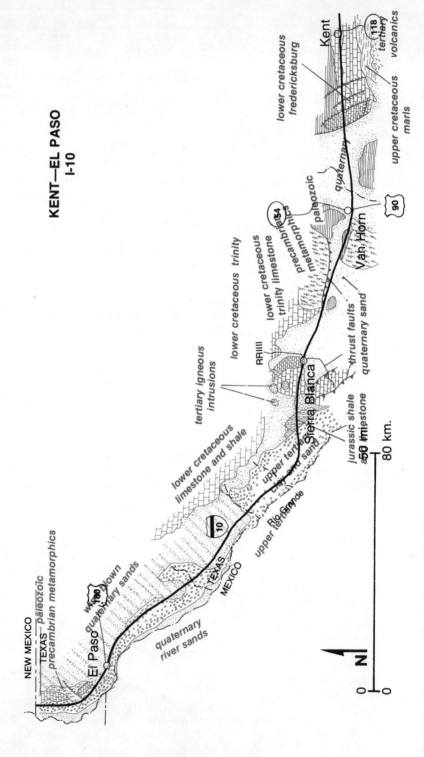

KENT—EL PASO
I-10

80 km.

68

interstate 10
kent—el paso

From Kent to El Paso, Interstate 10 provides some fascinating geology. As is logical from the point of view of those who build highways, but unfortunate from the point of view of the geologist, I-10 where possible stays on the open flat country. However, between Van Horn and just west of Sierra Blanca, it perforce crosses some very interesting geology. Elsewhere along the way a great deal more can be seen in the distance to either side.

The town of Kent is near the contact between the Trinity and Fredericksburg Groups of the lower Cretaceous System, but just to the north the Upper Paleozoic is exposed in the Apache Mountains. The highway continues westward for 15 miles (24 kilometers) in rocks of Cretaceous age which are repeated through a system of faults. Across each fault the western area is raised relative to that to the east. This is the southern expression of the Delaware Mountains which are related in origin to the frontal range of the Rocky Mountains.

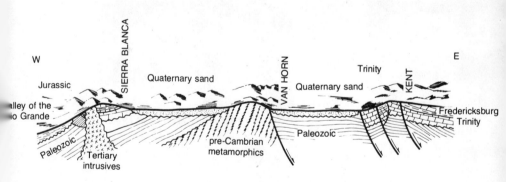

Cross section from Kent to Van Horn to Sierra Blanca along I-10.

Twenty miles (32 kilometers) farther west, I-10 drops again to the flat plains covered with Quaternary sands which were deposited only a few thousand years ago by flooding rivers and have since been shifted about by the prevailing westerly winds. Where water is available these plains have been extensively cultivated. Often the whole area is covered by airborne clouds of dust picked up from this disturbed surface.

Just east of Van Horn, the western limit of these plains is visible where additional faulting has brought the Paleozoic and older rocks to the surface. South of the highway, the Tertiary volcanic rocks of the Davis Mountains have receded into the background and been replaced by the limestones and shales of the upper Paleozoic Era. To the north are the much older rocks of the southern end of the Sierra Diablo Mountains.

Three miles west of Van Horn the roots of the Sierra Diablo or Devil's Mountains are exposed by a road cut into the highly folded Precambrian metamorphic rocks.

A closer view of these metamorphic rocks shows a pegmatite vein about two feet (60 cm.) thick composed of large crystals of quartz or feldspar.

The time elapsed between the formation of the metamorphic rocks and the deposition of the overlying limestones is of the order of two billion years.

The view to the south of the highway in this area provides a much closer look at the gently dipping upper Paleozoic limestone resting with pronounced angular unconformity on the steeply inclined metamorphic rocks of the Precambrian.

Ten miles (16 kilometers) west of Van Horn, I-10 enters a large flat valley filled by Quaternary flash-flood deposits of gravel, sand, and clay which extend to Sierra Blanca, where the limestone of the lower Cretaceous Period is again exposed. The southern limit of this valley is marked by a range of hills made up of westward-tilted rocks of the lower Cretaceous.

Immediately west of Sierra Blanca, the view to the west is dominated by pronounced conical hills of the Sierra Blanca just to the north of the highway.

The Sierra Blanca or "White Mountains" as seen from I-10 just west of the village of Sierra Blanca.

Looking northwestward from I-10, the town of Van Horn is barely visible to the left of the gap where pre-Cambrian metamorphic rocks are overlain on both sides by upper Paleozoic limestones.

These mountains are composed of igneous rock which, while still in a molten state, intruded the Cretaceous sediments while they were buried far below the surface. This took place during Tertiary time, some 40 million years ago, or at about the same time as the volcanoes were pouring forth the lavas which make up the Davis Mountains. The Cretaceous sediments are interbedded sands, shales and limestones. A road cut here on the south side of I-10 clearly shows how these rocks were locally altered or metamorphosed by the intense heat of the molten igneous rocks.

Interbedded sandstone, shale and limestone of Cretaceous age, partly metamorphosed by the intense heat in Tertiary time of igneous rock just beyond the fence line.

72

Ten miles (16 km.) west of Sierra Blanca, the highway cuts through the western edge of this Tertiary intrusion which makes up the rubble-strewn slopes to the north.

On the steep downward grade into the Rio Grande valley, I-10 passes through a poorly exposed belt of shale and limestone of lower Mesozoic Jurassic age. These sediments, which are about 200 million years old, form the core of the Malone Mountains to the north.

The seven-mile (11 kilometers) descent into the Rio Grande valley which starts about 12 miles (21 kilometers) west of Sierra Blanca is mostly covered by gravels washed down from the mountains to the east. It affords an excellent view across the sand dunes and river flats to the Cretaceous rocks making up the Sierra Madre in Mexico beyond the Rio Grande.

The first rock exposures seen after reaching the Rio Grande valley proper are horizontally bedded light tan or greenish grey clays of uppermost Tertiary or lowermost Quaternary age. These aptly named "bolson" deposits were formed some three million years ago, and are common in the semi-mountainous desert country of this part of Texas and adjoining Mexico. "Bolson" is Spanish for "big pocket" or "purse." The deposits were laid down where rivers entered land-locked valleys and left their load of mud and sand because the rate of evaporation was essentially equal to the rate of influx of water.

For the next 70 miles (113 kilometers) northwestward to El Paso, the highway follows the course of the river on these bolson deposits or

View westward along I-10 from the crest of one dune to the crest of the next. This is repeated almost ad nauseum between Sierra Blanca and El Paso.

on the sand dunes which cover them for long stretches. These dunes are partly stabilized by low vegetation, but partly still moving southeastward before the nearly constant winds which sweep down the valley. The crests of the dunes reach a height of 50 feet (15 meters) or more and follow each other at intervals of about a quarter mile (400 meters) providing a gentle roller-coaster profile to the highway.

The city of El Paso is on the flat valley fill of the Rio Grande surrounding the southern nose of the Franklin Mountains. The gap formed where this range is separated from the mountains of Mexico by the Rio Grande was a natural gate-way for the early Spaniards en route from Mexico to the north; hence the name "El Paso del Norte" or the Northern Passage.

The growth of El Paso is stopped abruptly by the steep, barren slopes of the Precambrian rocks of the Franklin Mountains.

The Franklin Mountains are a highly folded and faulted complex of Paleozoic and older rocks which rise abruptly from the flat valley as may be seen in the view of Comanche Peak from one of the principal thoroughfares in northwestern El Paso.

The growth of El Paso is stopped abruptly by the steep, barren slopes of the Precambrian rocks of the Franklin Mountains.

From El Paso to the New Mexico border, I-10 continues for 19 miles (31 kilometers) along the same young valley deposits interrupted only by isolated hills of Tertiary intrusive rocks.

SITES OF GEOLOGIC INTEREST

Franklin Mountains: A fine view of the geologic complexity of the Franklin Mountains and of El Paso and its environs can be had by a short drive from the central part of the city over Rim Road and Scenic Drive to Murchison Peak. The route passes through lower Paleozoic sediments into Precambrian metamorphic rocks with minor igneous intrusions; the geology is well described in publications of the El Paso Geological Society.

The look-out point on Murchison Peak provides an excellent view over downtown El Paso to the Rio Grande, the straight streets of the rectangularly laid-out Mexican city of Juarez, and the Cretaceous rocks in the mountains of Mexico.

For more information on connecting roads, see
Chapter V
> Interstate 10: Sheffield—Kent
> Interstate 20: Kent—Monahans
> U.S. 180: El Paso—Guadalupe Mountains
> Texas 54: Guadalupe Mountains—Van Horn
> Texas 118: Kent—Alpine—Marathon

The lookout point on Murchison Peak provides an excellent view over down-town El Paso to the Rio Grande, the straight streets of the rectangularly laid-out Mexican city of Juarez, and the Cretaceous mountains of Mexico.

interstate 20
kent — monahans

This is a part of Texas that can best be described by the quotation in the preface as "miles and miles of miles and miles." It is almost devoid of geologic interest, and is included only to fill in a part of the picture of the state. The first 15 miles (24 kilometers) to the east of Kent are in the Fredericksburg Group of the lower Cretaceous Period which is tilted gently eastward and overlain by the Quaternary sands which blanket much of West Texas.

These young river deposits continue across the Pecos River to isolated hills of Triassic or lowermost Mesozoic sands and clays. From here to Monahans the flat-lying Quaternary plains are dominant. The Triassic sandstones are responsible for the striking sand dunes just east of Monahans. Their exposure to the prevailing westerly winds provides a source of the grains of quartz that are blown into dunes.

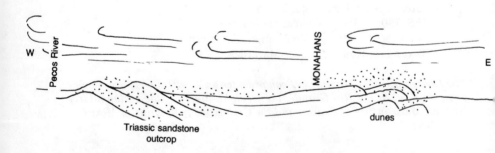

Over the course of many years the prevailing westerly winds have picked up the sand from the Triassic outcrop, transported it across the plains and dropped it to form the dunes.

76

u.s. 180
el paso — guadalupe mountains

Eastward from El Paso, U.S. 180 — which in this area is also U.S. 62 — runs for 20 miles (32 kilometers) in an almost perfectly straight line across the imperceptibly tilted Quaternary sands that fill the valley between the Franklin and the Hueco Mountains. These loose sands present a characteristic hummocky surface where the sparse vegetation of sage, tumbleweed, and creosote bush has prevented their being carried eastward by the prevailing winds. On the approach to the Hueco Mountains, sand dunes appear where the winds, upon being deflected upward, have dropped their burden of sand.

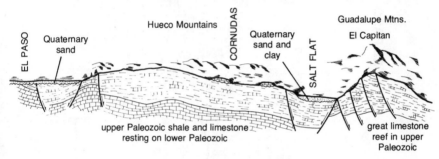

Cross section from El Paso to Guadalupe Mountains along U.S. 180.

The western foothills of the Hueco Range are made up of westward-tilted limestone and shale of the upper and lower Paleozoic Era where the uplift of the older rocks created a series of faults. Ten miles (16 kilometers) to the east, the terrain becomes more gently undulating. Here the surface is formed by the flat-lying shales and limestones of the Hueco Formation of Permian age which have been only slightly disturbed since their deposition in a shallow sea some 300 million years ago. "Hueco," pronounced "way-co," means hole or hollow in Spanish. It must have been given to these mountains because of the numerous shallow depressions caused by the dissolving of the limestone by underground waters.

This gently undulating surface extends past the crest of the range to a point 46 miles (74 kilometers) east of El Paso. There, resting on

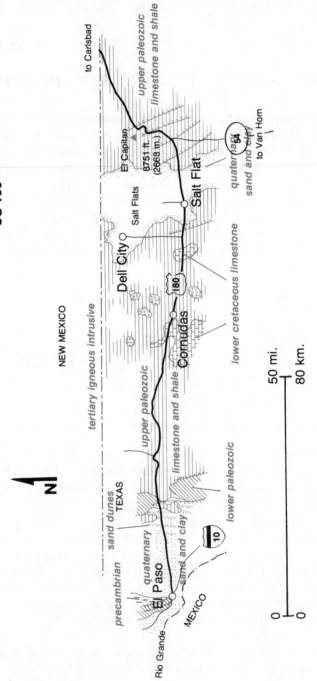

EL PASO—GUADALUPE MOUNTAINS
US 180

to Carlsbad

upper paleozoic limestone and shale

El Capitan
8751 ft.
(2663 m.)

Salt Flats

Salt Flat

quaternary
sand and clay

to Van Horn

54

Dell City

180

lower cretaceous limestone

Cornudas

NEW MEXICO

tertiary igneous intrusive

upper paleozoic

limestone and shale

lower paleozoic

N

precambrian

sand dunes

TEXAS

quaternary
sand and clay

El Paso

MEXICO

Rio Grande

10

50 mi.

80 km.

0

the upper Paleozoic, is a remnant or outlier of the white limestone deposited by the lower Cretaceous sea which covered the area about 100 million years ago. From this area, the view to the north is dominated by a group of prominent rounded hills formed by Tertiary igneous rocks which intruded the older sediments about 50 million years later. They are much more resistant to erosion than are the surrounding rocks, and thus remain as hills.

Hills of igneous rock which intruded the Paleozoic sediments during Tertiary time.

Ten miles (16 kilometers) to the east at Cornudas, which is a ranch rather than a town, the Cretaceous limestone has been completely eroded away, and the highway continues on the upper Paleozoic sediments to the village of Salt Flats. The flats are the bed of a vast land-locked lake which was once fed by springs near the Guadalupe Mountains to the north. As the impounded water was evaporated by the hot sun, great deposits of various salts accumulated. The springs are now nearly dry.

The salt deposits were once so highly valued that the issue of private vs. public ownership led to the destructive "El Paso Salt War" of 1877.

Across the glaring white salt flats, Guadalupe Peak, or El Capitan 15 miles (24 km.) to the northeast, and at 8751 feet (2668 m.) the highest point in Texas, forms an impressive background.

Just to the east of Salt Flat, and with El Capitan still in the background, is a typical state-maintained West Texas rest stop. Picnic tables are sheltered from the sun by a roof, and a stile across the barbed wire fence gives distressed travellers access to the nearest bush.

The imposing limestone reef of El Capitan from the junction with Texas 54 which goes southward to Van Horn.

The prominence of this peak is due to a combination of geologic factors. During Permian time, more than 300 million years ago, this part of Texas was covered by a tropical sea. A great reef — similar to the modern Great Barrier Reef off the east coast of Australia or the Bahamas east of Florida — developed where water depth and temperature favored the growth of abundant bottom-living marine life such as corals. The remains of these organisms formed a great mass of limestone. Uplift of the area at the end of Paleozoic time and more recently during Tertiary time, some 250 and 50 million years ago, caused extensive faulting, and the massive reef limestone resisted the subsequent erosion to maintain its topographic prominence. The development of this thick limestone reef in a section otherwise composed of thinner limestones and shale can be clearly seen in the photograph.

For more information on connecting roads, see

Chapter V
   Interstate 10: Kent—El Paso
   Texas 54: Guadalupe Mountains—Van Horn

FT. STOCKTON—BIG BEND NATIONAL PARK
US 385

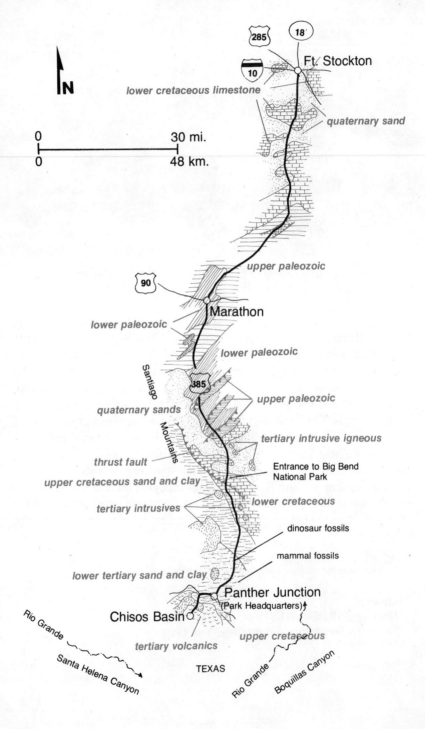

N

0   30 mi.

0   48 km.

285 *18* *10* Ft. Stockton

lower cretaceous limestone

quaternary sand

upper paleozoic

90 Marathon

lower paleozoic

lower paleozoic

385

upper paleozoic

quaternary sands

tertiary intrusive igneous

Santiago

thrust fault

Mountains

Entrance to Big Bend
National Park

upper cretaceous sand and clay

lower cretaceous

tertiary intrusives

dinosaur fossils

mammal fossils

lower tertiary sand and clay

Panther Junction
(Park Headquarters)

Chisos Basin

upper cretaceous

Rio Grande

tertiary volcanics

Santa Helena Canyon

TEXAS

Rio Grande

Boquillas Canyon

MEXICO

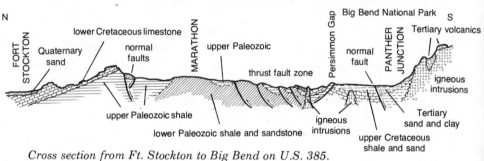

u.s. 385
fort stockton — marathon
— big bend national park

U.S. 385 provides the most direct route to the Big Bend National Park which is a major attraction for anyone travelling through West Texas. En route to the Park it offers an excellent look at some of the best exposed and most interesting geology in the state.

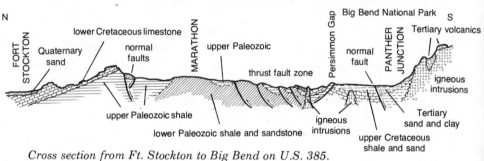

Cross section from Ft. Stockton to Big Bend on U.S. 385.

The geology along the route may be separated into three basic and distinct categories.

From Fort Stockton to Marathon, U.S. 385 crosses Quaternary age sand flats which fill the topographically low areas between the hills formed by gently northward-tilted lower Cretaceous limestones. These limestones were deposited some 100 million years ago by a broad sea that covered an area where the Paleozoic rocks that were deposited 500 to 200 million years earlier had been tilted and then eroded to form an irregular plain.

South of Marathon the geology becomes more complex, and the Paleozoic rocks have been steeply folded and faulted with only scattered remnants of the overlying Cretaceous rocks remaining. Midway between Marathon and the entrance to the Big Bend Park at Persimmon Gap, is an extensive zone of thrust faulting where the older rocks have moved upward and northwestward to overlie the younger rocks. This activity began around the end of Cretaceous time some 80 million years ago and resumed some 40 million years later during Tertiary time. It was accompanied by intrusions of molten igneous rock into the sediments.

South of Persimmon Gap, the geology is dominated by this igneous activity, and is further complicated by another system of thrust faulting in which the older rocks moved toward the *south*west to over-ride the younger rocks. This last fault system raised the Santiago Mountains which are prominent west of the highway for many miles. The mountainous nature of the countryside, the reason for the National Park, is due primarily to this Cretaceous and Tertiary activity.

Seven miles (11 kilometers) south of Ft. Stockton, U.S. 385 climbs gradually out of the valley-filling Quaternary sand, deposited by water and wind over the last few thousand years and into the flat-lying limestone hills of the lower Cretaceous. With minor exceptions where it drops into young valleys, it continues its gentle climb in Cretaceous rocks for another 24 miles (40 kilometers) to a point where the base of the Cretaceous rests unconformably on the more steeply tilted shale and limestone of the upper Paleozoic. Some minor faulting can be seen in this area where the Cretaceous has dropped down a few hundred feet.

W   E

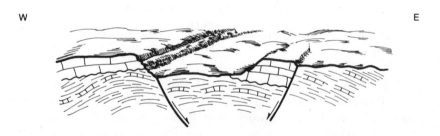

20 miles (32 km) north of Marathon; a block of Cretaceous limestone faulted down into Paleozoic shale and limestone across U.S. 385.

The highway continues southwestward in upper Paleozoic rocks for 15 miles (24 kilometers). Hills on either side are made of thick layers of shale separated by thinner beds of harder limestone and sandstone. Six miles (10 kilometers) northeast of Marathon, these rest on harder and more steeply folded sediments which were deposited in lower Paleozoic seas some 500 million years ago, and now form the core of the Marathon uplift. The most common rocks along the road to Marathon are very hard fine-grained, white, siliceous marine sediments known as chert or novaculite. In its pure form, this rock is widely used to sharpen fine steel cutting tools and therefore acquired its name from the Latin word for razor.

Within the first two miles (3 km.) to the south of Marathon the same is poorly exposed along the road side, but well exposed in the hills to the west. Where the slope of the hill side is very nearly the same as the tilt or dip of the rock layers, the white novaculite produces a scalloped design such as that seen 10 miles (16 km.) farther south.

From here southward, the highway crosses a series of thrust faults in which the lower Paleozoic rocks have been pushed upward toward the northwest to over-ride the upper Paleozoic rocks. This thrusting has resulted in the repeated stacking up of the same series of rocks through a zone several miles wide.

In an area starting 25 miles (40 kilometers) south of Marathon and extending well south of the Park entrance at Persimmon Gap, limestones of lower Cretaceous age rest with a strong angular uncomformity on the much older Paleozoic sediments. This is an excellent example of how the older rocks were folded and uplifted into mountains, and then eroded down to allow the Cretaceous sea to cover the area. After the deposition of the Cretaceous, the area was again raised above sea level and eroded until only remnants of the once wide-spread Cretaceous sediments now remain.

Paleozoic shales which rise abruptly from the Quaternary plain are tilted steeply to the right and away from the observer, and capped by only gently tilted limestones of Cretaceous age. Between the deposition of the Paleozoic shales and the deposition of the Cretaceous limestones, some 400 million years elapsed.

The Santiago Mountains dominate the view to the west. These mountains are composed of igneous rocks of Tertiary age. The lower hills in the foreground are lower Paleozoic sediments pushed upward and southwestward by the thrust fault which lies between.

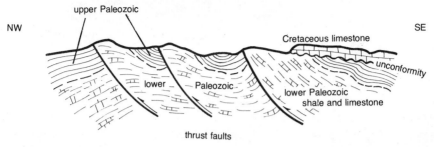

Sketch of thrust fault zone and unconformable overlap along U.S. 385 between Marathon and the Big Bend.

Within five miles (8 kilometers) of the entrance to the Big Bend Park at Persimmon Gap, U.S. 385 crosses a flat plain covered by loose rubble washed down from the surrounding hills of lower Cretaceous limestone. Jutting sharply upward from the plains, or from the limestone, is a series of higher and darker hills made of igneous rock. The molten magma rose into the sediments during Tertiary time some 40 million years ago. These intrusions are related to the great volcanic eruptions which once covered much of the area with lava flows.

Double Mills watering place with Tertiary igneous rocks intruded into the Cretaceous sediments.

A marker placed along the highway where it crosses this plain bears the testimony of the Texas State Historical Survey Committee to the importance of water in this arid area. Prehistoric artifacts have been found here, and history records that the water was used by Indians and Spaniards travelling northward from Mexico.

The Upper Paleozoic shales and Cretaceous limestones of the prominent hill just south of Persimmon Gap have been pushed up against the younger Cretaceous sediments that appear to the right.

Persimmon Gap, where U.S. 385 enters the Park, is a natural gap in the lower Cretaceous limestone hills which separate the Quaternary-filled valley to the north from the valley to the south which is filled with marine and river sediments of upper Cretaceous and lower Tertiary age.

The major thrust fault that is crossed just south of the Gap is the same one that raised the Santiago Mountains to the north. In this case, the movement of the rocks was southwestward with the older rocks on the northeast side pushed over the younger rocks on the southwest. Where the highway crosses the fault, lower Cretaceous limestones and upper Paleozoic shales are pushed up over the upper Cretaceous sediments. The chaotic deformation of the once horizontal layers is readily apparent in the hillsides.

From just south of Persimmon Gap, the traveller has his first good view of the Chisos Mountains 30 miles (50 km.) to the south.

From just south of Persimmon Gap, the traveller has his first good view of the Chisos Mountains 30 miles (50 kilometers) to the south. These mountains are composed of various intrusive and volcanic igneous rocks, and form the scenic as well as the geologic heart of the Big Bend National Park. The gently tilted sands and clays in the foreground were the beaches and tidal flats of the upper Cretaceous sea some 80 million years ago.

The Upper Cretaceous sediments yielded fossil remains of the Pterosaur, a giant flying reptile, that recently received nationwide publicity. Its skeleton is being studied and restored by the Univeristy of Texas at Austin.

About 17 miles (27 kilometers) south of Persimmon Gap the highway crosses a zone of steep faulting where the Tertiary sand and clay to the south dropped down against the upper Cretaceous rocks to the north. Just south of this fault zone an exhibit shows the types of dinosaurs that left their fossil remains in the Cretaceous clays and sands, and of mammals whose fossil bones have been found in the Tertiary river deposits here and to the south. The exhibit buildings are on the cross-bedded sandstone deposited by flooding rivers in which the mammal fossils are commonly found.

Cross-bedding is the result of the deposition of sand and mud by flowing currents — in this case water — when the rate of flow varies because of changes in weather conditions over a period of days or a great many years. The direction of the flow can be read from the shape of the layers. More rapid flow results in the deposition of larger rock fragments.

Southward from the fossil exhibit, the highway climbs steadily for ten miles (16 kilometers) through the Tertiary sediments until it reaches the main igneous complex of the Chisos Mountains at Panther Junction.

The Park Headquarters is located here, and a visit will add greatly to the understanding and enjoyment of the Park. The variety of maps and pamphlets available for inspection or purchase offer a wealth of information on all aspects of the Park. The geology of the Park is too complex and varied to be treated fairly here, and warrants the more complete coverage provided by some of the references listed in the bibliography.

A nine-mile (15 kilometer) drive from Panther Junction leads to the Chisos Basin, the geographic focal point of the Park. Three miles (5 kilometers) west of the Headquarters the road to the Basin branches off to the south and climbs quickly but easily for the next 5 miles (8 kilometers) before descending the last mile into the Basin.

View of Casa Grande Peak from the pass where the highway starts its descent into the Chisos Basin.

The prominent mesa-like peak is Casa Grande which is formed of nearly horizontal Tertiary lavas that flowed out onto the surface. The hills on either side are of igneous rock that crystallized far below the surface at a much earlier date.

For more information on connecting roads, see

Chapter V
   Interstate 10: Sheffield—Kent
   Texas 118, U.S. 90: Kent—Alpine—El Paso

View westward from the lodge at the foot of Casa Grande across the camping area and through The Window.

91

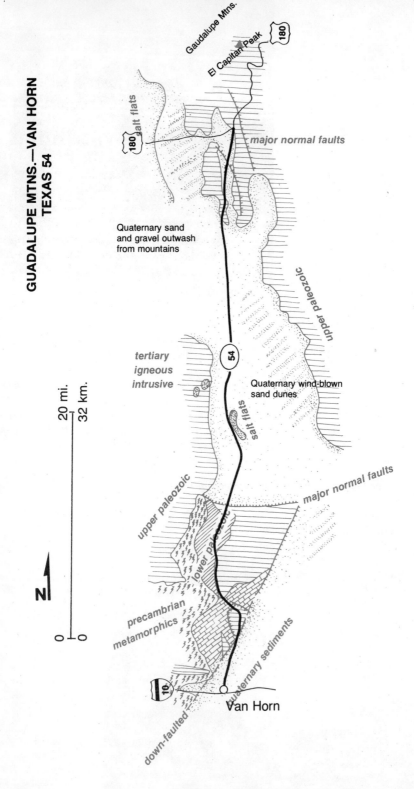

GUADALUPE MTNS.—VAN HORN
TEXAS 54

Gaudalupe Mtns.

180

El Capitan Peak

Gaudalupe Mtns.

major normal faults

salt flats

180

Quaternary sand
and gravel outwash
from mountains

upper paleozoic

*tertiary
igneous
intrusive*

54

Quaternary wind-blown
sand dunes

salt flats

20 mi.
32 km.

upper paleozoic

major normal faults

lower paleozoic

N

*precambrian
metamorphics*

0

quaternary sediments

10

down-faulted

Van Horn

texas 54
guadalupe mountains—van horn

More than three quarters of this route is along flat plains formed by sands and gravels deposited by flooding streams. They washed from the surrounding mountains during the last few thousand years. Paleozoic and older rocks that range in age from some 300 million to more than one billion years are superbly exposed in the surrounding mountains. The lack of moisture, which is responsible for the scarcity of vegetation and the consequent lack of soil development makes the geology readily visible from the highway.

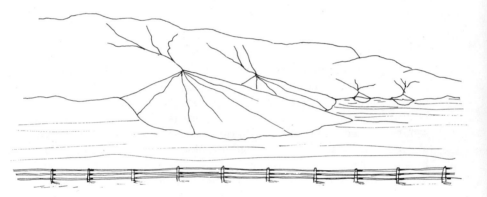

Alluvial fan formed at foot of ridge.

The same situation prevails for 30 miles (50 kilometers) to the south. The Quaternary sand and gravel deposits are interrupted east of the highway by a dried-up lake bed or salt flat which once was part of a large salt lake just southwest of the Guadalupe Mountains.

Thirty-three miles (53 kilometers) south of its junction with U.S. 180, Texas 54 leaves the Quaternary valley and enters a rocky stretch. The hills to the west show upper Paleozoic sediments resting with pronounced angular unconformity on metamorphic rocks of Precambrian age.

Just south of U.S. 180, the view to either side of Texas 54 shows pronounced ridges of gently tilted Upper Paleozoic shale and limestone rising sharply above the Quaternary plain. Streams have washed great quantities of boulders and gravel from the mountains to form the low, rounded hills that lie between the ridges and the flat plains.

The rocky hills in the foreground are Precambrian quartzites or metamorphosed sandstones, the background ridge is Paleozoic red shales capped by the massive upper Paleozoic limestone. The difference in the angle of tilt of the bedding of Paleozoic and the older rocks is readily seen in the photo. Here there is a major unconformity separating sediments of two different ages spanning a time interval of about one billion years. The older rocks are brought to the surface by a great normal fault that crosses the valley from east to west and dropped the younger rocks several hundred feet.

The rocky hills in the foreground are Precambrian quartzites or metamorphosed sandstones; the background ridge is Paleozoic red shales.

In this area a very interesting phenomenon can be seen. To the west of the highway and in the right-center of the photo, Paleozoic limestone has slid down the hill into the area of the older shale. This modern event was caused by the erosion of the valley, the weight of the Upper Paleozoic limestone, and the weakness of the underlying Paleozoic shale.

The ten miles (16 kilometers) of Texas 54 just north of Van Horn crosses a complexly faulted zone of rocks ranging in age from the more than one billion year-old Precambrian to yesterday's wind and water deposits.

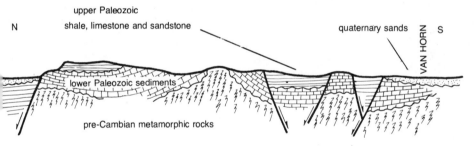

Complex normal faulting just north of Van Horn.

For more information on connecting roads, see

Chapter V
    Interstate 10: Kent—El Paso
    U.S. 180: El Paso—Guadalupe Mountains

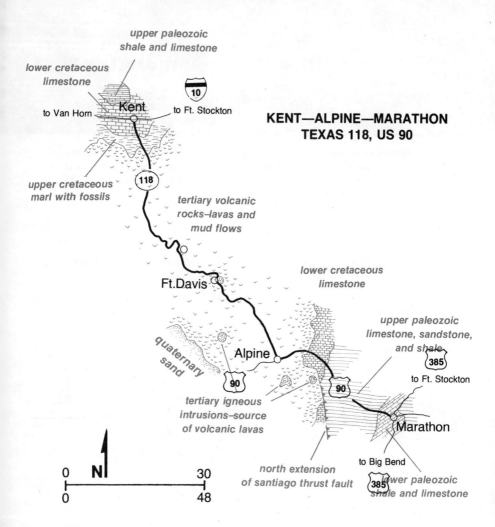

118
90

upper paleozoic
shale and limestone

lower cretaceous
limestone

10

to Van Horn · **Kent** · to Ft. Stockton

**KENT—ALPINE—MARATHON
TEXAS 118, US 90**

upper cretaceous
marl with fossils

118

tertiary volcanic
rocks–lavas and
mud flows

Ft.Davis

lower cretaceous
limestone

upper paleozoic
limestone, sandstone,
and shale

385

to Ft. Stockton

quaternary
sand

Alpine

90

90

Marathon

tertiary igneous
intrusions–source
of volcanic lavas

to Big Bend

north extension
of santiago thrust fault

lower paleozoic
shale and limestone

385

N

0		30
0		48

texas 118, u.s. 90
kent—alpine—marathon

From Kent to Alpine, Texas 118 goes through some of the most scenically interesting country in West Texas. The entire route is dominated by the Tertiary basaltic lavas and volcanic mud-flows that make up the Davis Mountains.

The volcanic rocks occur in thick, nearly horizontal layers that vary in color from dark grey, where the exposures are fresh, to all shades of brown and red where the iron content has oxidized. The cliffs and hillslopes almost always present a rough, blocky appearance that distinguishes them from the smoother slopes and more regular layering of the sedimentary rocks around the margins of the Davis Mountains.

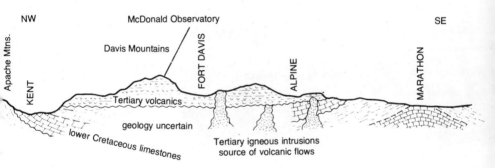

Cross section from Kent to Alpine to Marathon.

The molten rock reached the surface through a series of fault-induced fractures in the underlying sediments. Some of the volcanic vents can be seen in the more isolated peaks.

Two miles (3 kilometers) south of Kent, the highway leaves the lower Cretaceous limestones and passes through the upper Cretaceous marl where fossil oyster-like forms can be collected. Five miles (8 kilometers) farther it reaches the base of the Tertiary volcanic rocks that once covered most of this part of Texas. They are still preserved here in the Davis Mountains. These mountains differ from most in that they are not the result of a great up-lifting and folding of the older rocks, but rather of a gentle down-warping of the earth's crust. Fractures related to the Santiago thrust zone allowed molten rocks from far below to reach the surface in a series of volcanic eruptions that began some 50 million years ago and culminated some 25 million years later. These volcanoes erupted vast quantities of basaltic lavas and associated rocks. The Davis Mountains stand high because the lavas are more resistant to erosion than the surrounding sediments.

The McDonald Observatory, maintained and staffed by the University of Texas, is on one of the highest peaks of the Mountains and affords good views of the area.

Looking southward from McDonald Observatory. Twin Mountains on the skyline mark one of the volcanic vents from which the lava came. The darker lava caps the higher hills.

For the first ten miles (16 kilometers) eastward from Alpine on U.S. 90, Tertiary lava forms the hills to the south where it rests on lower Cretaceous limestone.

Columnar fractures of one of the basalt lava flows. During cooling, the horizontal layer of lava fractured with a vertical pattern, and subsequent weathering has given it the appearance of a series of closely-stacked vertical columns.

The dark basaltic rocks to the left are part of a "stock" where magma hardened in the vent through which the lava reached the surface.

A road cut on the north side of the highway a few miles farther east, exposes a remarkable view of the Cretaceous limestone on top of the upper Paleozoic rocks.

The Glass Mountains north of the highway are made up of upper Paleozoic rocks, and just before reaching Marathon, the road enters the lower Paleozoic rocks that form the heart of the Marathon Uplift.

The hammer in the center of the picture marks the contract, and just to the right is a conglomerate layer made up of fragments of the Paleozoic rocks which were broken and redeposited by the advancing Cretaceous sea. This contact represents the passage of 150 million years.

For more information on connecting roads, see
Chapter V

north central texas

Throughout most of Paleozoic time, from 600 to 300 million years ago, most of North Central Texas was covered by seas which advanced from the west and deposited great thicknesses of sands, clays and limestones. With the uplift of the Llano-Burnet region in Central Texas, much of the area raised above sea level to form the Bend arch which extends northward through this part of the state.

About 150 million years ago, the Cretaceous seas advanced from the east, or what is now the Gulf of Mexico, to again cover the entire area with limestone. The rejuvenated uplift of Central Texas and the Bend arch caused the seas to retreat again. Most of the Cretaceous rocks have since been removed by erosion to expose the upper Paleozoic sediments which now form the surface in most of North Central Texas. In general the rocks were only slightly tilted away from the Bend arch, and thus are now exposed over wide areas. Erosion of the highlands has removed only the upper or younger layers of the Paleozoic. No rocks older than Pennsylvanian or upper Carboniferous Period are exposed.

The upward-arching of the Paleozoic rocks was responsible for many of the oil fields found during the infancy of the industry in the first decades of this century. The oil "boom" was felt over much of North Central Texas.

interstate 20
big spring — abilene

Big Spring is on the 3 to 10 million-year-old river sands that form the surface of most of the High Plains to the north and west. For a few miles eastward, I-20 stays on the edge of the plains, but the Triassic and Cretaceous hills can be seen to the south where the young sand cover has been eroded away.

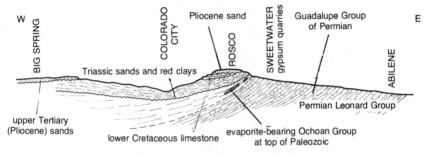

Cross section from Big Spring to Abilene.

The eastern limit of the Pliocene sands forms the scarp or "Cap Rock" that marks the edge of the Plains north of here, but where it is crossed 15 miles (24 kilometers) east of Big Spring, the scarp is only a few feet of strongly cross-bedded sandstone resting unconformably on the red clays and sands of the Triassic Period.

These Triassic sediments, which were deposited on a land surface near a shallow sea some 200 million years ago, continue for about 35 miles (56 km.) to beyond the crossing of the Colorado River at Colorado City.

101

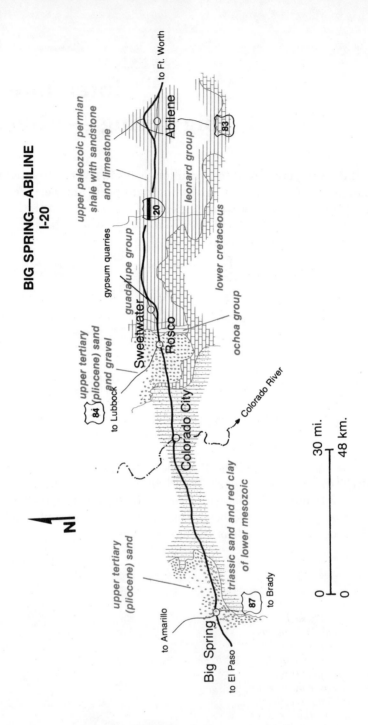

BIG SPRING—ABILINE
I-20

upper paleozoic permian
shale with sandstone
and limestone

leonard group

lower cretaceous

gypsum quarries

guadalupe group

ochoa group

Abilene

83

20

Sweetwater

Rosco

upper tertiary
(pliocene) sand
and gravel

84

to Lubbock

Colorado City

Colorado River

triassic sand and red clay
of lower mesozoic

upper tertiary
(pliocene) sand

to Amarillo

Big Spring

87

to Brady

to El Paso

to Ft. Worth

N

30 mi.

48 km.

0

0

These Triassic sediments, which were deposited on a land surface near a shallow sea some 200 million years ago, are exposed for about 35 miles (56 kilometers) to beyond the Colorado River at Colorado City. As the highway climbs the gradual slope from the river, it crosses an unconformable contact from the red Triassic rocks into the overlying white limestone of the lower Cretaceous which is some 100 million years younger. This belt of limestone, which is readily apparent because of its steeper slopes and the color change from red to white, is less than 2 miles (3 kilometers) wide. Then it disappears beneath a remnant of the Pliocene sand with an unconformity or hiatus denoting the passage of nearly another 100 million years.

The town of Rosco is built on the Pliocene cap. Just to the east, the road drops into much older red clay and sand of the Triassic. The Cretaceous limestones were completely removed by erosion before the Pliocene sands were deposited. This relationship is shown on the cross section.

From here to Sweetwater, I-20 passes rapidly downward through the eastern vestiges of the Triassic sediments and of the Ochoan Series of the uppermost Paleozoic — which contains important deposits of salt west of here — into the Guadalupe Series of the Permian Period of the upper Paleozoic. Unfortunately, none of these rocks is well exposed along the highway.

Just east of Sweetwater, white beds of gypsum and anhydrite in the dark red sandy clays of the Permian are well exposed in a creek bed just south of I-20. In this area they are mined extensively and processed for building materials such as sheetrock.

The upper part of the Guadalupe Series was deposited in a sea where the rate of evaporation was so high that the salts dissolved in the water were deposited in crystalline form on the sea bottom. In this case the most common mineral was calcium sulfate which was deposited as white to pink layers of gypsum or anhydrite. It is extensively quarried just east of Sweetwater where it is processed to manufacture various building materials such as wall-board. The white layers of gypsum and anhydrite interbedded with the darker red sandy clays can be seen in a creek bed just south of I-20 and east of Sweetwater.

From here to Abilene, the highway continues slowly downward through the Guadalupe Series and the underlying Leonard Series of the Permian. The countryside is generally flat, except for the low hills to the south where the horizontal Cretaceous limestones lie unconformably on the upper Paleozoic sediments.

The low hills on the horizon are Cretaceous limestone resting unconformably on the red sandy clay of the Permian.

interstate 20
abilene — fort worth

From Abilene I-20 continues eastward in the predominantly clay series of the lower Permian Leonard Group for 10 miles (16 kilometers). Then it climbs upward geologically as well as topographically into an erosional remnant or outlier of the lower Cretaceous Trinity Group which continues almost to Baird. This is a near-shore deposit that marks the invasion 100 million years ago of the Cretaceous sea onto the eroded surface of upper Paleozoic red sandy clay deposited 200 million years earlier.

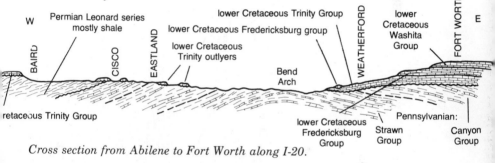

Cross section from Abilene to Fort Worth along I-20.

The lower-most or oldest of the Cretaceous sandstones are composed of angular fragments of the older rocks. They are overlain by fossiliferous limestones deposited later as the marine environment became established.

The hammer is imbedded in the red clays of the Permian Period; the overlying sandstones are Cretaceous.

105

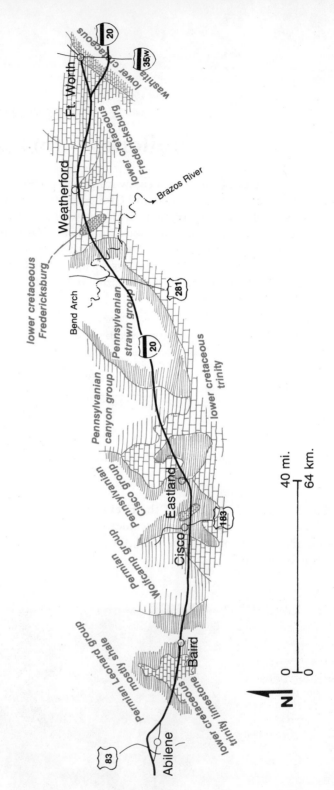

ABILENE—FT. WORTH
I-20

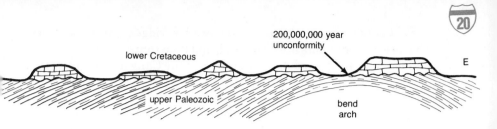

lower Cretaceous

200,000,000 year
unconformity

E

upper Paleozoic

bend
arch

Section along I-20 just east of Eastland showing lower Cretaceous limestone unconformably overlapping tilted upper Paleozoic sediments of Pennsylvanian age.

A similar geological situation prevails for most of the distance between Abilene and Fort Worth. I-20 very closely follows the unconformable contact between the upper Paleozoic red clay and the overlying Cretaceous sandstone and limestone in what would have been almost a sea-level route 100 million years ago. The Paleozoic rocks were gently folded into the broad Bend arch, and are tilted westward to a point roughly midway between Eastland and Weatherford where the crest of the arch is reached and the tilt reverses to the east. The Paleozoic surface was eroded to an almost horizontal plain which was covered by the Cretaceous sea. The Canyon Group, or the middle part of the Pennsylvanian, is well exposed in road cuts just east of Eastland where it consists of sandstone and limestone with abundant fossils that show that it was deposited near the shore-line of the Paleozoic ocean.

Typical roadside exposure of the Pennsylvanian sandstones and limestones. Such exposures often offer good fossil collecting.

107

East of here, the highway crosses two low ridges where the lower Cretaceous sediments are preserved, and then continues in the inter-bedded limestone, sandstone, and shale of the Canyon Group and the underlying Strawn Group of the Pennsylvanian to where these older rocks disappear under the lower Cretaceous overlap just east of the Brazos River. Throughout this stretch, the sky-line to the east, west and south shows conical and mesa-like hills of the lower Cretaceous resting on the old Paleozoic surface.

From Abilene to the crossing of the Brazos River, all of the rocks belong to the Trinity or lowest Cretaceous series, and carry few recognizable fossils. East of the Brazos, the entire countryside is covered by Cretaceous, and the young Fredericksburg Group forms the higher hills until, in the center of Fort Worth, the almost imperceptible eastward tilt of the rock layers has allowed the youngest of the lower Cretaceous sediments — the Washita Group — to be preserved.

The Fredericksburg is the most abundantly fossiliferous of the lower Cretaceous units. Where it is exposed five miles (8 kilometers) east of the Brazos River, it offers an excellent opportunity to collect many types of fossil remains of both bottom-living and free-swimming shell fish. The fossils in the photo were collected within a few minutes drive along I-20; the lower Cretaceous ammonite and oysters in the upper part of the photo are some 100 million years old — the upper Paleozoic corals, crinoids and clam-like brachiopods below are 200 million years older.

For more information on connecting roads, see

Lower Cretaceous fossils above the roler and upper Paleozoic forms below.

108

u.s. 87
big spring—san angelo—brady

Although this route crosses sedimentary rocks ranging in age from the 500 million-year-old lower Paleozoic just east of Brady to the 5-million-year old Pliocene at Big Spring, it is remarkably devoid of any tectonic or structural disturbance. Throughout the entire area, the originally horizontal layers of rock have, in that span of one-half-billion years, been only slightly tilted westward so that the geological progression from Big Spring to Brady is slowly and gradually downward into older sediments. There are marked gaps or unconformities in the geological record at the base of the upper Paleozoic, the base of the Cretaceous and the base of the Pliocene, but the tectonic disturbances that caused these were nothing more than near-vertical uplift with slight westward tilting. Erosion which followed each period of uplift allowed the deposition of successively younger rocks on relatively flat surfaces.

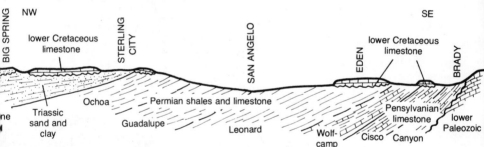

Cross section along U.S. 87 from Big Spring to Brady.

The pattern of the outcrops, as seen on the map, shows how the rivers have cut through the younger rocks into the older ones below. The older rocks are exposed along the valleys and the younger rocks generally form the higher elevations. This simple pattern changes abruptly near Brady where the uplift of the Central Texas Llano-Burnet area complicates things.

Big Spring is on the southeastern edge of the wide-spread upper Tertiary Pliocene sands that cover much of the High Plains. It derives

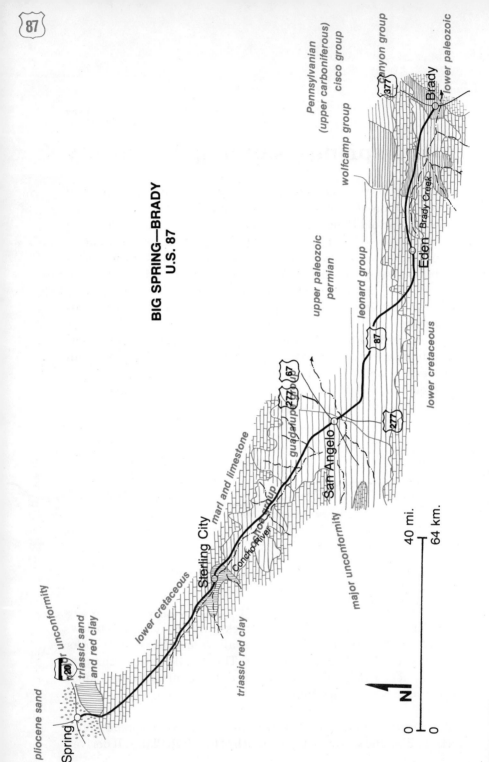

BIG SPRING—BRADY
U.S. 87

110

its name from the fact that in the early days of settlement of the area, it had the only fresh water for more than 50 miles (80 kilometers) in any direction. This water emerged in springs from the base of the Pliocene sands where they rested on relatively impervious clays deposited during the Triassic Period.

Immediately south of Big Spring, the sands have been eroded away to expose the reddish brown sandy clay and grey sandstone of the Triassic. Within five miles (8 kilometers) of the city, the Triassic sedimentary rocks disappear beneath lower Cretaceous limestone and shale. These sediments continue for most of the 43 miles (69 kilometers) to Sterling City, where the Triassic reappears.

Through this stretch of Cretaceous rocks, it is interesting to note the repeated change in vegetation. Where the Cretaceous is primarily shale, the predominant vegetation is the light green mesquite; the dark green juniper or cedar favors the limestone ridges. The color pattern clearly shows the geology. Much of the mesquite has been intentionally killed. These drouth-accustomed trees send their roots downward to several times their own height, taking water which might otherwise nourish the grass which feeds the cattle.

From Sterling City to San Angelo, the highway follows closely along the course of the Concho River. Erosion has stripped off the

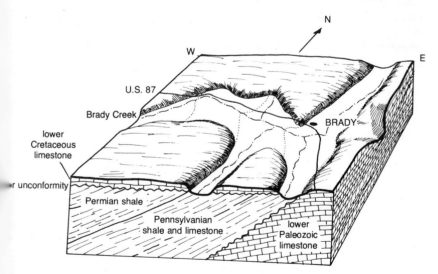

Major unconformities and effect of stream erosion on surface geologic expression near Brady.

Cretaceous sediments and exposed progressively older layers of the Triassic and Permian Periods. The hills on either side of U.S. 87 clearly show how the Cretaceous sea covered the gently tilted older rocks.

East of San Angelo, the highway gradually climbs the divide between the drainage area of the Concho River and that of Brady Creek, which flows by the town of Brady and eventually reaches the San Saba River. The town of Eden is near the crest of this divide. It is on the lower Cretaceous sediments which rest unconformably on the lower part of the Permian. From here to the town of Brady, the highway follows Brady Creek where it has eroded through the Cretaceous to expose the base of the Permian and the underlying Pennsylvanian limestone in the valley. The hills to the north and south are still capped by Cretaceous sediments.

At Brady the geology, and therefore the topography, change abruptly to that of the Central Texas hill country, where Paleozoic and older rocks appear.

For more information on connecting roads, see

u.s. 281
lampasas — stephenville

Between Lampasas and Stephenville, U.S. 281 stays entirely in rocks of the lower Cretaceous Trinity and Fredericksburg Groups. The layers are nearly horizontal, and the total change in elevation of the surface is only a few hundred feet. The only change in the observed geology is where the rivers have eroded through the Fredericksburg into the Trinity.

The highway runs very nearly along the axis of the Bend arch as it extends northward from the Llano-Burnet uplift of Central Texas. The regional tilting of the Paleozoic rocks, which are completely covered by the Cretaceous in this area, is to the east and west away from this axis, and the overlying Cretaceous sediments have remained very nearly horizontal just as they were deposited more than 100 million years ago.

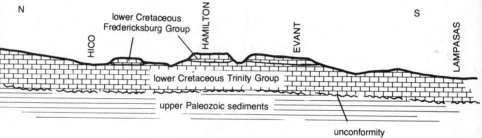

Section from Lampasas to Stephenville.

When Central Texas and the Bend arch were being raised some 80 million years ago to end deposition of the Cretaceous, the rivers that flowed southeastward to the receding sea established much the same courses they follow today. Erosion removed the upper Cretaceous rocks and much of the lower Cretaceous which had covered the area. Only the lowermost or Trinity Group and part of the overlying Fredericksburg Group remain.

The Trinity is made up of irregular layers of thick limestone and shale that form the rugged, but patternless, topography of the val-

LAMPASAS—STEPHENVILLE
U.S. 281

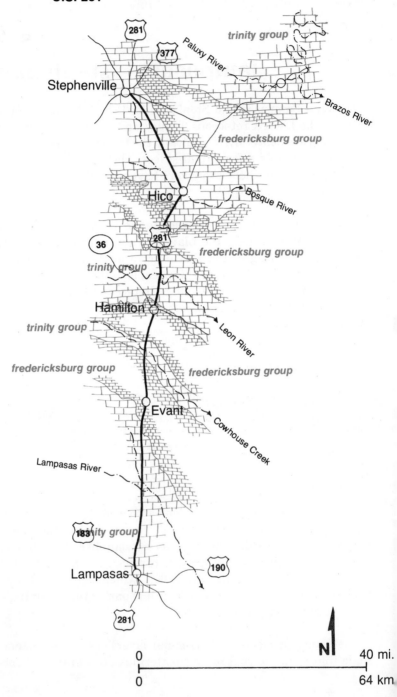

trinity group

Paluxy River

Stephenville

Brazos River

fredericksburg group

Hico

Bosque River

fredericksburg group

trinity group

Hamilton

Leon River

trinity group

fredericksburg group

fredericksburg group

Evant

Cowhouse Creek

Lampasas River

trinity group

Lampasas

| 0 | | 40 mi. |

| 0 | | 64 km |

N

leys. In the intervening higher areas between the valleys, the Fredericksburg is preserved because its upper part consists of very hard limestone that protects the lower shales and marls from erosion. The bedding or layering of the rocks in this series is very regular and sharply defined, giving the surface a distinctive layered pattern.

In this view overlooking the valley of Cowhorse Creek just north of Evant, the foreground and background are the basal shales and marls of the Fredericksburg which contain abundant fossil remains of oysters, clams, and snails that thrived in the tidal flats and coastal waters. The rocks in the intervening valley are the limestone and shale of the Trinity Group.

The reason for the preservation of these softer sediments is evident. The flat-topped hills are capped by the hard limestone of the upper part of the Fredericksburg Group which gives rise to the distinctive topography.

Hard limestone of the Fredericksburg caps the hills overlooking the valleys of softer rocks.

Dinosaur Tracks: The 30-mile (48-kilometer) sidetrip to Dinosaur Valley State Park near Glen Rose from U.S. 281, is worth the effort.

The time of deposition of the Trinity Group of the lower Cretaceous Period, more than 100 million years ago, coincided with the reign of the giant reptiles known as dinosaurs — monarchs of the earth. The conditions that prevailed in what is now North Central Texas were ideal for these great beasts whose name is derived from the Greek words for terrible lizard. The warm shallow seas with low-lying coastal areas yielded ample plant growth to feed the marine and terrestrial vegetarians who provided the diet for the meat-eaters. The muddy and slimy bottoms of these coastal waters and tidal flats have long since solidified into marl and limestone which preserve their footprints.

Trinity limestone and marl as exposed along the banks of the Paluxy River near Glen Rose. The layers contain many dinosaur footprints formed when the rocks were soft limy muds.

Tyrannosaurus on the left,
Brontasaurus on the right.

This park was established by the state along the Paluxy River just west of Glen Rose, and can be reached by a 30-mile (48-kilometer) drive eastward along U.S. 67 from Stephenville, or a 25-mile (40-kilometer) drive northeastward along Texas 220 and U.S. 67 from Hico. From the crossing of the Paluxy River at the western outskirts of Glen Rose, Park Road 59 leads 4 miles (6 kilometers) northward to the park.

Here the top of the Trinity contains sandstone which weathers reddish-brown, but this gives way downward to the interbedded limestone and marl typical of the banks of the Paluxy River.

Just within the park, life-sized replicas of the carnivorous dinosaur, Tyrannosaurus, and the long-necked herbivorous Brontosaurus upon which he fed, give an impressive view of the types of reptiles that abounded at the time the Trinity sediments were deposited.

Track of a smaller dinosaur preserved in the limestone that forms the bed of the Paluxy River.

This photograph, courtesy of the Texas Memorial Museum, was taken when the waters of the Paluxy River were diverted during the earlier investigation of the area. The tracks on the right to center were made by a plant-eater who walked on all four feet; those on the left were made by a meat-eater who walked on his hind feet with a stride of as much as 12 feet (4 m.).

Most of the tracks that may now be seen in the bed of the Paluxy River were made by smaller members of the dinosaur family.

For more information on connecting roads, see

Chapter IV
    U.S. 281: San Antonio—Lampasas
Chapter VI
    U.S. 281: Stephenville—Wichita Falls

u.s. 281
stephenville—wichita falls
—oklahoma

For 8 miles (13 kilometers) north of Stephenville, U.S. 281 climbs through the limestone of the Trinity Group of the lower Cretaceous until it reaches the crest of the divide between the valley of the Bosque River and that of the Brazos river to the north. At the divide there is an abrupt change between the flat-topped hills of the nearly horizontal Cretaceous limestones to the south and east, and the lower, less regular topography created by erosion of upper Paleozoic sandstones, shales and limestones that extend more than 100 miles (161 kilometers) to the north and west.

The highway continues in lower Cretaceous rocks for another 15 miles (24 kilometers). Nine miles (14 kilometers) south of the Brazos River, the flat limestones of the Cretaceous rest unconformably on the gently tilted sediments of the upper Paleozoic Era, deposited some 200 million years earlier.

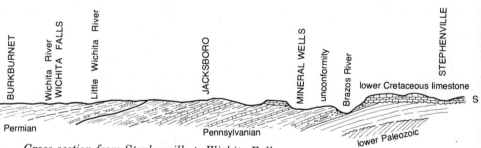

Cross section from Stephenville to Wichita Falls.

Before deposition of the upper Paleozoic sediments, some 400 million years ago, the surface of the land had been eroded to a nearly flat plain, which the Pennsylvanian seas flooded from the west. Rivers from the east deposited their load of rock fragments along the coastal area, building deltas of gravel, sand and clay. Reefs and banks of limestone and limy mud and sand formed in the off-shore waters.

119

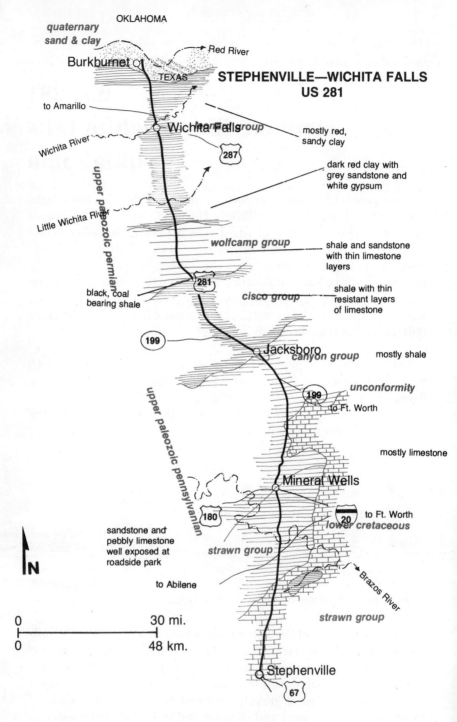

OKLAHOMA

quaternary sand & clay

Red River

Burkburnett

TEXAS

STEPHENVILLE—WICHITA FALLS US 281

to Amarillo

Wichita Falls

Wichita group

mostly red, sandy clay

Wichita River

287

dark red clay with grey sandstone and white gypsum

upper paleozoic permian

Little Wichita River

wolfcamp group

shale and sandstone with thin limestone layers

281

black, coal bearing shale

cisco group

shale with thin resistant layers of limestone

199

Jacksboro

canyon group

mostly shale

upper paleozoic pennsylvanian

199

unconformity

to Ft. Worth

mostly limestone

Mineral Wells

180

20

to Ft. Worth

lower cretaceous

sandstone and pebbly limestone well exposed at roadside park

strawn group

Brazos River

to Abilene

strawn group

N

0 — 30 mi.
0 — 48 km.

Stephenville

67

Rocks exposed near the Brazos River belong to the Strawn Series, the oldest Pennsylvanian rocks in this area. They consist of quartz pebbles embedded in a matrix of dirty limestone showing that they accumulated where the river deltas encroached on the limy muds off-shore. Good exposures of these sediments may be seen at a roadside park five miles (8 kilometers) north of the Brazos River.

Here the joints, or vertical fractures in the slightly tilted rock layers have allowed the surface waters to erode them into a jumble of large blocks.

The Strawn Group continues to Mineral Wells, although it slowly changes to limestone and shale deposited farther offshore from the mouths of the rivers. The road heads out to the Pennsylvanian sea as it goes north.

At Mineral Wells, the Strawn Group is overlain by the younger Pennsylvanian Canyon Group which was deposited as mud and clay on the shallow sea bottom after the earlier high country to the east had been nearly leveled by erosion. These softer rocks form a generally smoother land surface largely devoted to agriculture and extend 30 miles (48 kilometers) northward to Jacksboro. For more than half this distance, the western edge of the Cretaceous hills can be seen east of U.S. 281 where they lap onto the Pennsylvanian.

At Jacksboro the uppermost and youngest of the Pennsylvanian sediments, known as the Cisco Group, overlie the Canyon Group. The Cisco is mostly shale which was deposited in a shallow, muddy sea. It also includes many thin layers of limestone which contain abundant fossil remains of shell-fish and plants that lived in the coastal waters.

These thin, erosion-resistant limestone layers control a series of low ridges gently tilted northwestward.

Twenty miles (32 kilometers) northwest of Jacksboro, the shales of the Cisco Group contain enough plant remains to be black and carbonaceous, or coal-like. The sea had slowly receded westward, allowing coastal swamps to develop and nourish abundant plant life. Layers of coal are widespread in this area and were mined locally until the discovery of oil put the coal mines out of business. As liquid fuels become scarce, limited coal-mining may resume in the future.

For the next 23 miles (37 kilometers) U.S. 281 crosses sand and shale with layers of limestone until it reaches the Little Wichita River 15 miles (24 kilometers) south of Wichita Falls. The contact between the upper Pennsylvanian Cisco Group and the Lower Permian Wolfcamp Group is along this stretch of road. However, the depositional conditions and thus the exposed rocks were so similar that the change in age is not readily evident.

Just south of the crossing of the Little Wichita River, these sediments are overlain by the distinctive rocks of the middle Permian Leonard Group. These consist of dark red clay with cross-bedded grey sandstone and white gypsum.

The rocks were deposited after the seas had disappeared from the area. The sands accumulated in river channels, and the gypsum formed by evaporation of the remaining salty water.

This type of rock yields poor soil, and the countryside is covered by cactus and low scrubby brush that supports cattle. It continues past Wichita Falls almost to Burkburnet where it is overlain by the modern flood deposits of the Red River which forms the border with Oklahoma. Winds sweeping across the Red River have picked up some of the river sands, depositing them as sand dunes which are especially prominent on the Oklahoma side.

Between Mineral Wells and the Red River, the traveller is seldom out of sight of gas or oil fields or their related installations. The fields produce almost entirely from the lower part of the Pennsylvanian sediments.

For more information on connecting roads, see

Chapter VI

high plains

This geographic region of Texas benefits from having a descriptive name while most other regions refer to directions such as "Central," "West," and "East." The commonly used local names of "Llano Estacado" or staked plains, and "Panhandle" are apt. However, with a mean elevation of 3500 feet (1067 meters), a surface whose regional slope is only 8 feet per mile (1.5 meters per kilometer), and a surface relief that is only locally perceptible, "High Plains" fits the area admirably.

The surface of the High Plains is a vast sheet of sands and clays deposited in the late Tertiary Pliocene Period less than 10 million years ago. Flood waters and winds distributed coarse and fine rock fragments over the area and levelled any topograhic differences that existed.

Areas where the modern rivers have eroded through this cover offer the only "windows" to the underlying geology. Thus it is the valleys rather than the usual mountains that provide the geologic story. Even there, the geology is only a partial glimpse into the past.

The complexity of the deep-seated geology is known from the results of the many deep wells that have been drilled in the area in search of oil and gas, but is beyond the scope of this book. However, an event that made national news in June 1978 may help to illustrate it. An earthquake—not devastating, but distinct—was felt from San Angelo to New Mexico and from Lubbock southward to old Mexico. The epicenter, or point on the Earth's surface directly above the cause of the tremor, was just north of Odessa.

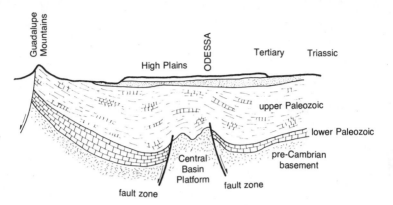

Schematic section through southern High Plains showing the Central Basin Platform as a location of earth movements causing earthquakes.

The fundamental forces that caused the Central Basin Platform to exist and have kept it growing upward for the last one-half-billion years are still active. The weight of the tens of thousands of feet of sediments that have accumulated on the flanks of this platform is sufficient to cause the rocks to slip downward along the previously existing fault zones. This movement is sporadic rather than gradual, and a sudden movement far below the surface caused the shock waves that were felt as an earthquake.

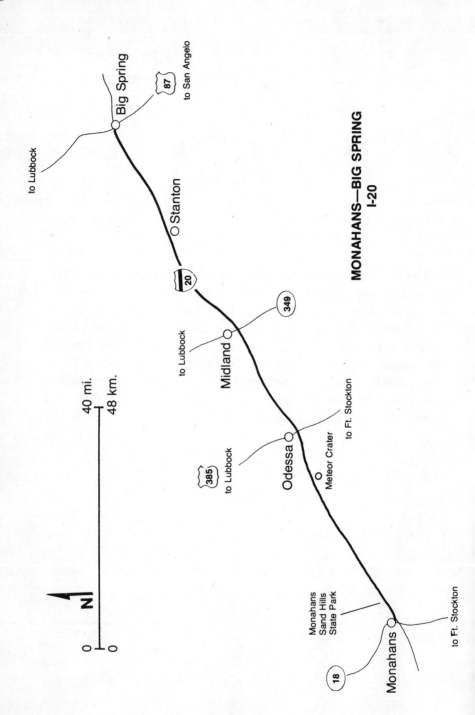

MONAHANS—BIG SPRING
I-20

interstate 20
monahans—odessa—big spring

In the West Texas section, the countryside between Kent and Monahans was described as "miles and miles of miles and miles." That phrase is equally applicable to the part of I-20 from Monahans to Big Spring.

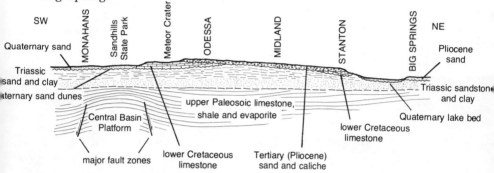

Cross section from Monahas to Big Spring along I-20.

Monahans is on the broad plain of Quaternary sand that covers most of the valley of the Pecos River for more than 100 miles (161 kilometers). In the course of the last few thousand years in this arid climate, the prevailing winds from the west have shifted and redeposited these sands. Just east of Monahans, the highway crosses a belt of active dunes built where the winds are still depositing sand.

The eastern limit of these dunes is a 10-mile (16 kilometers) strip of lower Cretaceous limestone and sandstone which disappears just west of Odessa beneath the Pliocene or upper Tertiary sand and clay that covers most of the High Plains. They extend past Midland about half way to Big Spring. There they have been removed by erosion to expose the Cretaceous limestones and the underlying red clay and sand of the Triassic Period near the town of Stanton.

The 20-mile (32 kilometers) stretch from just east of Stanton to the outskirts of Big Spring, is covered by lower Quaternary or Pleistocene sand deposited by the flood waters during the rainy period that coincided with the melting of the ice-sheets that periodically covered much of North America during the glacial epoch of the past million years.

At Big Spring, I-20 is again on the Pliocene sand near the south-easternmost edge of the High Plains.

SITES OF GEOLOGIC INTEREST

Monahans Sandhills State Park: The entrance to the park is on the north side of I-20 just five miles (8 kilometers) east of Monahans. The belt of active dunes is where the prevailing winds are depositing sand picked up from the Quaternary plains and Triassic sandstone to the west. The State maintains picnic grounds along several miles of paved road that wind through the area. This provides excellent views of how the wind-blown sands build the ever-shifting dunes.

The winds carry the quartz sand up the long, gentle slope to the sharp crest, where it drops down the steeper eastern side.

As in much of western Texas, oil is produced from the Paleozoic sediments thousands of feet below, by pumping wells similar to this one within the park.

Odessa Meteor Crater: Within the outcrop zone of the lower Cretaceous marls, and only 10 miles (16 kilometers) southwest of Odessa, a long-since filled, but still visible, crater with an up-turned rim of the otherwise flat limestone shows where a large meteorite hit the Earth's surface perhaps 25,000 years ago. This may be easily reached by turning southward from I-20 at the "Meteor Crater" sign, and following the signs along the minor ranch roads for about two miles (3 kilometers).

The site has been thoroughly investigated, and at one time was developed and maintained as a tourist attraction. It has now been abandoned.

This view looking westward across the crater which is over 500 feet (150 m.) in diameter, shows the pumping wells of a Paleozoic oil field as the only current activity.

The view southward along the east rim of the crater shows the originally horizontal limestone layers sharply up-turned by the impact of the meteor.

For information on connecting roads, see

interstate 27, u.s. 87
amarillo—big spring

This flat stretch of highway gives an unsurpassed view of the High Plains as they exist today. With the exception of a few miles near Big Spring where Quaternary lake deposits are crossed, the entire route is on the nearly horizontal sands and clays of the Pliocene Epoch. They have lain almost undisturbed since they were deposited three million years ago.

Between Amarillo and Plainview, this surface is almost 100% irrigated and cultivated, but south of Plainview it is much the same as when the European explorers and settlers first saw it. From Lamesa to Big Spring, the many fields that produce oil and gas from various levels in the underlying Paleozoic sediments are so closely spaced that they give the impression of an almost continuous producing field.

Most of the changes in the surface appearance of the High Plains have occured within the last 50 years. It takes little imagination to see the countryside as Chad Oliver, in *The Wolf Is My Brother,* describes it from the point of view of an Indian 100 years ago.

"It was big country, open country, and it seemed to hold few secrets as it rolled away under the pale blue vault of the sky.
"It was a hard land, but it was not truly barren. There were buffalo grasses and grama grasses, and pale green yuccas that thrust stalks of white blossoms into the air...
Above all it was the big sky and the great white fireball of the sun."

Invisible from this highway, but never distant more than 50 miles (80 kilometers) to the east, is the rim of the High Plains where the Pliocene cover has been eroded away in a sharp escarpment to expose the hundreds of millions of years older Triassic and Paleozoic rocks. Where the larger streams which have their headwaters on the High Plains have cut through this "cap-rock" of the Pliocene, they often have cut steep-sided gorges.

to Oklahoma
51 mi. (82 km.)

to Dalhart — **Dumas**

pliocene

27
87
40
287

triassic

upper paleozoic

quate...

Canadian River

*pliocene sand,
gravel & caliche*

North Fork
Red River

Amarillo

Glenrio

Shamrock

upper paleozoic

Salt Fo...
sandy clay Red Rive...

Canyon

Prairie Dog Fork
Red River

triassic

upper paleozoic

Tex. 217
to Palo Duro Canyon

HIGH PLAINS

AMARILLO—BIG SPRING
I-27, US 87

OKLAHOMA—AMARILLO—NEW MEXIC...
I-40

AMARILLO—DUMAS—OKLAHOMA
US 87, US 287

Plainview

pliocene

0   8...
0   129

Lubbock

Brazos River

*lower cretaceous
sand & gravel*

Tahoka

Ranch Road 213

*lower cretaceous
sand & limestone*

Lamesa

*triassic sand and
red clay*

Colorado River

*quaternary
lake deposits*

Big Spring

to Abilene
*lower cretaceous
limestone*

to Kent   to San Angelo

N

The Prairie Dog Fork of the Red River has cut the most spectacular and most easily accessible of these just to the east of the town of Canyon 16 miles (26 kilometers) south of Amarillo. This is known as Palo Duro Canyon, of which a part has been developed as a State Park. It figures prominently in local folklore and history; and, again with the permission of the author, I quote from *The Wolf Is My Brother·*

"Palo Duro was concealed by its very unexpectedness. The flat plains seemed to stretch on endlessly; it was against common sense that a great invisible gash could cut through that hard sun-baked earth. If a man knew about Palo Duro he might be able to sense that shadowed break in the land when he was still several miles away. If he did not know, he could almost ride over the edge of the canyon before he saw it."

SITES OF GEOLOGIC INTEREST

Palo Duro Canyon: Texas 217 leads 12 miles (19 kilometers) eastward from I-20 at Canyon to the entrance to Palo Duro State Park where 6 miles (10 kilometers) of paved roads give the visitor an inside view of 800 feet (244 meters) of the rocks immediately below the surface of the High Plains. Here erosion by Palo Duro Creek which becomes the Prairie Dog Fork of the Red River provides a quick look at 300 million years of geologic history from the upper part of the Permian Period through the Triassic and the Pliocene Epoch of the Tertiary Period.

Section through Palo Duro Canyon; Texas 217 East of Canyon.

Sediments of the upper Paleozoic Permian Period form the lower and more rounded slopes of the canyon, and consists of red shale and sandstone with streaks and layers of white gypsum up to 10 feet (3 meters) thick. They were largely deposited by rivers, but the presence of the gypsum indicates the sporadic existence of land-locked water bodies that dried up to deposit their dissolved salts of calcium and sulfate.

133

The Triassic rocks form the steeper middle slopes of the canyon wall, and are maroon, lavender and yellow shale and sandstone with streaks of white. These give the distinctive "layer-cake" appearance to the middle and upper part of the canyon wall, and were deposited under similar conditions following a geologically brief period of erosion. The uppermost part of the Triassic section consists of hard sandstone and cemented gravel or conglomerate which were deposited during a time of torrential flooding, and now form well-defined cliffs.

After the deposition of the Triassic sediments, there is a gap of some 200 million years in the geologic history of this area. During part of this time the area was covered by Cretaceous seas, but the resulting deposits were eroded away before the deposition of the Pliocene gravel, sand and clay that now make up the top 100 feet (30 meters) or so of the canyon wall.

View eastward across Palo Duro Canyon from the rim near the Park entrance. The entire horizon is the Pliocene sandstone and caliche; the middle flattopped hills are Triassic sandstone resting on the Permian shale which has been eroded in vertical gulleys.

The Triassic sandstone cliffs and varicolored shale and sand as seen from the red Permian shale of the canyon floor.

134

W

E

Pliocene sand

Triassic sandy clay

Schematic section near Tahoka across U.S. 87 and along R.R. 213.

Tahoka Cretaceous Hills: Near the town of Tahoka, 29 miles(47 kilometers) south of Lubbock, the otherwise almost perfectly flat horizon is broken to the east and west of U.S. 87 by low isolated hills that rise about 50 feet (15 meters) above the Pliocene plains. These are made up of cemented angular gravels and sands and are remnants of the first sediments deposited near the shoreline of the lower Cretaceous sea 100 million years ago. Locally remnants which have survived erosion now stick up as residual hills on the surrounding plains.

Ten miles (16 kilometers) south of Tahoka or three miles (5 kilometers) north of O'Donnell, Ranch Road 213 offers the opportunity to drive one mile west of U.S. 87 and see these old, coarse gravel deposits where they have been excavated for road-building material.

For more information on connecting roads, see

Chapter VI
   Interstate 20: Big Spring—Abilene
   U.S.87: Big Spring—San Angelo—Brandy
Chapter VII
   Interstate 20: Monahans—Big Spring

Cretaceous gravel hill as seen from U.S. 87; the foreground is Pliocene sand and clay.

interstate 40
oklahoma—amarillo
—new mexico

Interstate 40 enters the Texas Panhandle from Oklahoma within what is properly a part of the North Central Texas region of predominantly upper Paleozoic sedimentary rocks. From the border to Shamrock — 14 miles or 23 kilometers — the highway closely follows the southern edge of the broad valley of the North Fork of the Red River, and alternates between the red sandy clay of the upper Permian Period and the river deposits of the Quaternary Period.

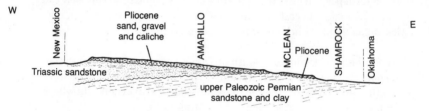

Section across the Texas panhandle along I-40.

Three miles (5 kilometers) west of Shamrock the Permian contains layers·of hard white anhydrite and gypsum up to 6 feet (2 meters) thick that result in more pronounced topographic relief. These erosion-resistant layers form the low ridge south and west of Shamrock.

Nine miles (15 kilometers) west of Shamrock, a gentle rise marks the eastern edge of the Pliocene sheet of gravel, sand and clay that forms the surface of most of the High Plains. These nearly horizontal, three million-year-old river floodplain deposits cover the entire route westward to Amarillo except for a small "window" near McLean where they have been eroded away to expose the cross-bedded red sandstone of the uppermost Permian.

The Pliocene cap-rock continues westward from Amarillo to within 10 miles (16 kilometers) of the New Mexico border. There the tributary streams of the Canadian River have worn it away to expose the sandstone and gypsum-bearing clay of the Triassic Period which is absent near Shamrock.

For more information on connecting roads, see

Chapter VII
Interstate 27, U.S. 87: Amarillo—Lubbock—Big Spring
U.S. 287: Amarillo—Stratford—Oklahoma

u.s. 287
amarillo—stratford
—oklahoma

Along this route, the only interruption of the flat Pliocene surface that forms the High Plains is provided by the valley of the Canadian River whose waters have cut through the cap-rock and the underlying Triassic sandstone into the Permian sandy clay and anhydrite. This topographic feature is locally known as the "canyon" or the "breaks" of the Canadian, which gives a clear indication of the importance to the residents of any break in the flatness of the High Plains.

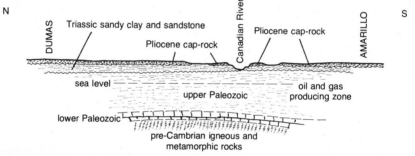

Section across Canadian River along U.S. 287.

In the cross section the surface relief is grossly exaggerated in order to allow the topographic and geologic changes to be shown. The photograph taken from near the southern rim of the "canyon" better illustrate its size relative to the vast extent of the Plains.

Looking northeastward across the Canadian River. Foreground and the horizon are Pliocene gravel; the rock ledges along the river are Triassic sandstones.

View up the Canadian River near the U.S. 287 highway bridge. The river bed is cut into the red sandy clay of the Permian Period which is overlain by Triassic clay and sandstone and capped by the Pliocene.

For information on connecting roads, see

Chapter VII
    Interstate 27, U.S. 87: Amarillo—Lubbock—Big Spring
    Interstate 40: Oklahoma—Amarillo—New Mexico

southwest texas

This part of Texas includes areas that do not fit into any of the other regions. The part south and west of San Antonio — the "Brush Country" and "Pear Flats" — merge imperceptibly eastward with the Gulf Coast; the "Edwards Plateau" west and north of Junction blends into West Texas, the High Plains, and North Central Texas. In some respects it epitomizes the definition of Texas as that part of the Earth that was left over and which God gave to Texas because he didn't know what else to do with it.

The Balcones Fault Zone which forms the natural dividing line between the Gulf Coast and East Texas on the east, and Central and North-Central Texas on the west, is much less pronounced southwestward from San Antonio. Nevertheless, it still serves to separate Southwest Texas into a lower Tertiary zone toward the Gulf of Mexico and a Cretaceous zone to the north and west.

The dominant geologic feature is the Rio Grande embayment along which the present Rio Grande flows. It has in various ways influenced the deposition of sediments for the last 200 million or so years.

The absence of any striking topographic features in this area reflects the general simplicity of the surface geology. From the flat Cretaceous plains of the Edwards Plateau to the present Gulf Coast, the gentle regional tilt of the rocks toward the coast is interrupted only by minor faulting and attendant folding that is rarely visible at the surface. Along the trend of the Balcones Fault Zone in the region of Uvalde, volcanoes which erupted in early and middle Tertiary time contributed ash to the coastward sediments. But only gently rounded hills of dark basalt now mark their presence. The Devil's River and the

Pecos River have cut spectacular canyons into the Cretaceous limestones just northwest of Del Rio, but even these are now partly submerged under water backed up by the Amistad dam. Except for such erosional features along the major streams, the Edwards Plateau is an essentially featureless plain that supports cactus, low brush, and a few cattle.

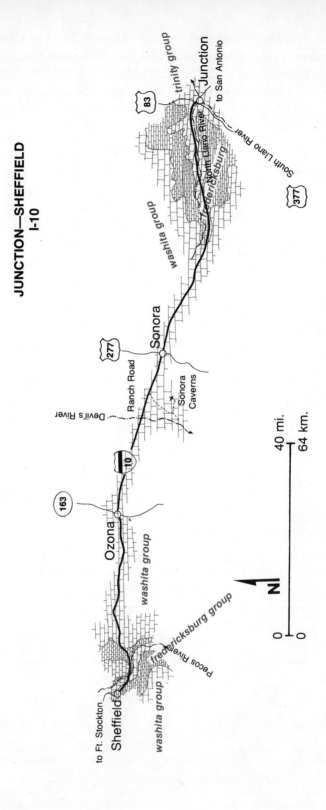

JUNCTION—SHEFFIELD
I-10

interstate 10
junction—sonora
—sheffield

The town of Junction, at the confluence of the three main branches that form the Llano River, is very near the base of the lowermost Cretaceous Trinity Series. Within 20 miles (32 kilometers), I-10 climbs slowly upward both topographically and geologically out of the Trinity, through the Fredericksburg Group and into the Washita Group as it follows up the valley of the North Llano River toward Sonora.

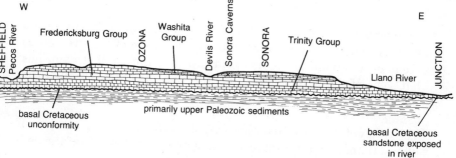

From this point to where the highway reaches the drainage area of the Pecos River just east of Sheffield, it continues through the flat-lying limestone and marl of the Washita. For 70 miles (113 kilometers) the traveller has a view of a few hundred feet of the Washita

Typical countryside in Washita Group.

Close-up of roadcut in Washita marly limestone showing fossil remains of plants and animals that lived in the Lower Cretaceous sea.

sediments that have changed only by hardening from the time when they were deposited as limy muds on the bottom of the Cretaceous ocean over 100 million years ago. Erosion by the small streams has left some of the harder layers as hills, and the construction of the highway has made possible a close view of the rocks.

The valley of the Pecos River just east of Sheffield offers a good view of almost the entire section of rocks that make up the lower Cretaceous.

The Pecos River valley as seen looking northward from the rest area on the eastern rim. The cliff-like rim of the canyon is in the Washita; the more gradually sloping middle walls are in the Fredericksburg, and at the base the river has cut down into the Trinity.

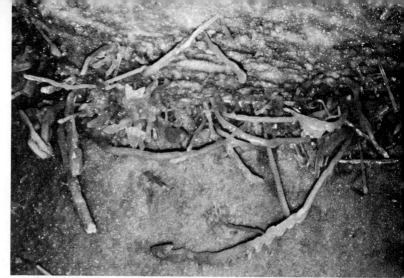

Helictites

SITES OF GEOLOGIC INTEREST

Sonora Caverns: Within 10 miles (16 kilometers) west of Sonora, signs are posted along I-10 advertising the Sonora Caverns. For the traveller who has two or three hours to spend, these caves provide a rewarding short side trip. Well marked and maintained paved roads lead to the entrance a few miles south of I-10.

The caverns, in common with most extensive caves, are the result of solution of the limestone by underground waters. In this case, the limestone is in the Washita Group that forms the youngest part of the

Helictites with "butterfly"

Fringed ribbon formed along ceiling fissure.

nearly horizontal lower Cretaceous. The Sonora Caverns are privately maintained as a tourist attraction, and in some ways are more interesting than many of the better-known caves. In some parts the slowly seeping water is still building intricate structures of stalactites, which hang down from the roof, and stalagmites which build up from the floor. Other fascinating forms include helictites which are fragile tubes that in apparent defiance of the laws of gravity extend outward at any angle from the cave walls and ceiling. They are formed of minerals deposited by evaporation of water that seeps through the drinking-straw-like tubes by capillary action.

For information on connecting roads, see

Chapter IV
    Interstate 10: San Antonio—Kerrville—Junction
    U.S. 290: Austin—Fredericksburg—Junction
Chapter V
    Interstate 10: Sheffield—Kent

interstate 35
san antonio — laredo

San Antonio straddles the Balcones Fault Zone in limestone and marl of Cretaceous age, but near the southern city limit, I-35 crosses into the lower part of the Tertiary and progresses slowly upward in these Eocene sands and clays for the entire distance to Laredo.

Between Pearsall and the Frio River the highway passes through oil fields that produce from the underlying upper Cretaceous sediments. For the remainder of the route little of geological variation is evident excepting changes in soil color from dark red between the Frio and the Nueces where the rocks are rich in iron, to light buff and grey where the concentration of iron minerals is much lower. The oxidation or rusting of the iron is responsible for the red color.

In general this is the mesquite and chaparral covered cattle-raising "brush country" with no marked change in the vegetation except along the Nueces River. There, the alluvial soil supports tremendous growths of prickly-pear cactus to form the "pear-flats" that figure in many of O. Henry's tales of the area.

The almost straight line of the highway between Pearsall and Laredo attests to the lack of topographic relief that results from the lack of important change in the geology.

For information on connecting roads, see

Chapter IV
    Interstate 10: San Antonio—Kerrville—Junction
    Interstate 35: Georgetown—Austin—San Antonio
    U.S. 281: San Antonio—Lampasas
Chapter X
    Interstate 10: Orange—Houston—San Antonio
    Interstate 37: San Antonio—Corpus Christi
    U.S. 83: Brownsville—Laredo

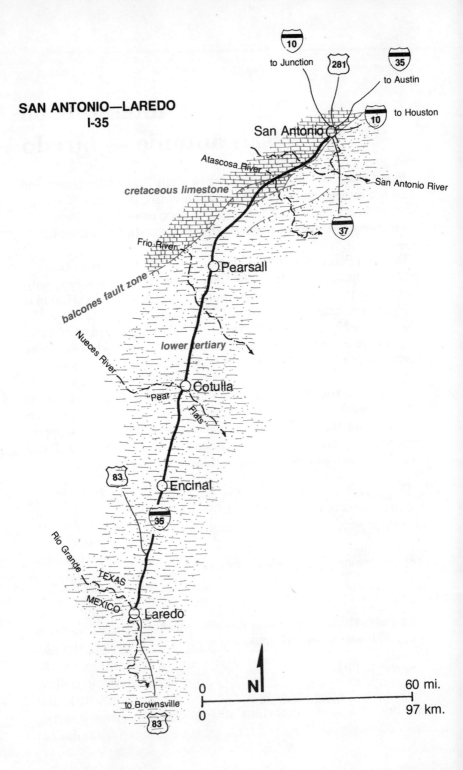

SAN ANTONIO—LAREDO
I-35

to Junction

to Austin

to Houston

San Antonio

Atascosa River

San Antonio River

cretaceous limestone

Frio River

balcones fault zone

Pearsall

Nueces River

lower tertiary

Cotulla

"Peat Flats"

Encinal

Rio Grande

TEXAS

MEXICO

Laredo

to Brownsville

N

0   60 mi.

0   97 km.

east texas

This portion of Texas is a geologic and geographic entity distinct from the rest of the State, although its western and southern boundaries are difficult to define sharply. In a broad sense, it consists of a great basin or embayment where large volumes of clays and sands accumulated during upper Cretaceous and lower Tertiary time from 100 to 40 million years ago as the shoreline of the sea slowly retreated eastward and southward. These sediments were carried toward the ocean by the ancestors of the present rivers because of the regional uplift of the areas to the west and north.

This relative geological movement corresponds, on a continent-wide basis, with renewed uplift of the ancient Appalachian Mountains and the birth of the Rocky Mountains. On a state-wide basis, it was marked by the fracturing of the rock layers that resulted in the Balcones Fault Zone that roughly marks the western boundary of East Texas, and the Mexia-Talco Fault Zone that crosses the northern part. The southern boundary of East Texas is more arbitrarily chosen to correspond approximately with the area where the younger and thus more modern Tertiary sediments now occur.

To the non-geologist traveller, the identity of East Texas is apparent with a similar degree of gradual but definite change. The rocky hills along the western side are replaced by the rolling black-land prairies where the upper Cretaceous limy shale is exposed, and these in turn by the low sandy hills and red clay valleys characteristic of the lignite and iron- bearing rocks of the lower Tertiary. The scrubby junipers or cedars of the limestone country give way to grassy plains dotted with small oaks where they have not been cleared for agriculture or grazing, and then to the great forests of conifers and hardwoods that culminate in the "Piney Woods" of deep East Texas.

Coastward from the western part of East Texas the rock layers are tilted only slightly to the east and south so that younger and younger rocks form the surface. Minor local interruptions are present, but the gentle regional tilt is such that only a few thousand feet of sediments deposited over the course of a few 10's of millions of years are exposed.

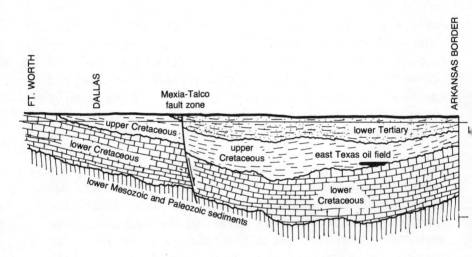

Section across northern part of east Texas.

interstate 30
dallas—texarkana

Fifteen miles (24 kilometers) east of Dallas, I-30 crosses the Hubbard Reservoir which was formed by the damming of the Trinity River where it flows through marls and clays of the Upper Cretaceous age. Just east of Greenville the highway crosses the Mejia-Talco Fault Zone which is similar to and here sub-parallel to the Balcones Fault Zone. Like the Balcones Fault Zone, it was caused by the relative subsidence or dropping down of the rocks to the south and east which caused the layers to break in a series of faults, and the younger ones on the southeast side to be preserved from erosion. About six miles (10 kilometers) east of this fault zone the route enters lower Tertiary clays and sands. They accumulated where the rivers from the northwest flowed into the sea 60 or 70 million years ago. From here, the trend of the rock layers and of the fault zone swings sharply eastward, and the highway roughly follows the geological trend. The minor folds and displacement of the rock layers have given rise to numerous small oil fields. The oil is produced from upper Cretaceous sands a few thousand feet below the surface.

Near Sulphur Springs, I-30 reaches the lower Tertiary Wilcox Formation which consists primarily of sand and sandy clay deposited just inland from the coast some 50 million years ago. The dominant reddish color is due to the oxidation of the iron in the sands. These sediments are economically important in East Texas because they contain extensive beds of low-grade coal or lignite, the carbonized remains of vegetable matter which grew as dense thickets and forests in the coastal swampy areas lying between the stream channels.

The lignite deposits occur in a somewhat sporadic belt from southwest of San Antonio to Texarkana and have been mined—also sporadically — since the 19th century. The growing shortage of oil and gas as sources of energy has renewed interest in these deposits,

EAST TEXAS
GEORGETOWN TO OKLAHOMA
I-35
DALLAS TO TEXARKANA I-30

0   100 mi.

0   161 km.

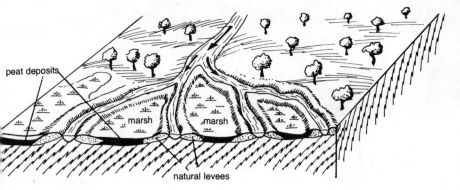

Diagram of a lignite-forming delta-marsh system.

and they are now being mined in numerous areas by modern open-pit or strip-mining methods. One such mine is just north of Winfield between Mount Vernon and Mount Pleasant. Some of the operations can be seen by taking a short side trip.

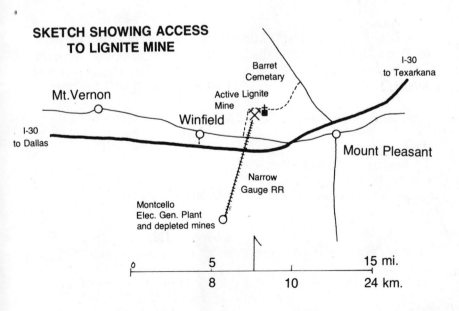

Bucket crane or drag-line with 300 foot (100 m.) boom removing overburden to reach lignite about 30 feet (10 m.) below surface.

The mining operations are closed to the public in the interest of safety, but can be seen by taking the Winfield exit from I-30 and following the sketch map. The dirt road to the Barrett Cemetery is rough but passable, and offers a good view of the mining operations. The mining companies respect the tradition of hallowed ground, and neither disturb cemeteries nor restrict public access to them. The operators are required by state law to restore the mined areas after depletion of the lignite, and generally do an excellent job. In many cases, the value of the land for agriculture and grazing is greater after restoration than in its undisturbed state.

I-30 continues in lower Tertiary rocks to Texarkana with little change except for the broad Quaternary alluvial deposits of the Sulphur River.

At Lone Star, 26 miles (42 kilometers) southeast of Mount Pleasant on Texas 49 and U.S. 259, the Lone Star Steel Co. mines low-grade iron ore from the lower Tertiary sands, and fabricates steel pipe and building materials.

For information on connecting roads, see

Chapter VI
    Interstate 20: Abilene—Fort Worth
Chapter IX
    Interstate 35: Georgetown—Dallas—Oklahoma

Huge truck hauling lignite to the plant. The road to the Barrett Cemetary passes through the culvert over which the truck is passing.

interstate 35
georgetown—dallas
—oklahoma

This stretch of I-35 crosses rocks of Cretaceous age with the softer sediments of the upper Cretaceous predominating and responsible for the relatively subdued topography. The weathering and decomposition of these rocks produces the dark, fertile soil of the Black and Grand Prairies, some of Texas' most productive agricultural and grazing land.

Cultivation on the Upper Cretaceous prairie near Hillsboro.

Between Austin and Waxahachie the highway closely follows the Balcones Fault Zone, and between Georgetown and Temple is on the up-lifted side, and thus is almost entirely in the older lower Cretaceous limestone.

Between five and 15 miles (8 and 24 kilometers) north of Georgetown, several odd flat-topped hills can be seen. These may at first glance appear to be man-made, but are actually "shell-banks" which were built up of shell fragments and other detritus in elongate heaps by near-shore currents in the lower Cretaceous sea some 120 million years ago. Their prominence today is due to their being more resistant to erosion than the surrounding softer rocks.

Near Hillsboro, where west I-35 branches off to the northwest to reach Denton by way of Fort Worth, the flat agricultural terrain is the shale of the upper Cretaceous Woodbine formation. One hundred miles (161 kilometers) to the east, in the Tyler-Longview area, some of the sediments deposited during this same time interval were sand rather than mud because that area was near the shoreline of the upper Cretaceous sea. These sands are the reservoirs from which most of the oil in the great East Texas fields is produced.

From Waxahachie through Dallas to Denton, east I-35 continues over progressivly older upper Cretaceous rocks. Between Dallas and Lewisville they are covered by the Quaternary deposits of the Elm Fork of the Trinity River which are less than 10 thousand years old. From Denton northward to the Oklahoma Border at the Red River, the highway follows without significant geologic change along the upper part of the lower Cretaceous.

For information on connecting roads, see

gulf coast

The Gulf Coast of Texas is the geologically youngest region of the state and extends eastward and southward from the Balcones Fault Zone near San Antonio and Austin to Louisiana and the Gulf of Mexico.

For the last 50 million years the Gulf Coastal Plain has subsided as areas to the west and north were raised. The weight of the tremendous amount of sand and clay deposited by the southeastward flowing rivers has caused part of the subsidence. During this time, the shoreline of the Gulf gradually receded until it reached its present position. This process is continuing today as sediments continue to accumulate; the great chain of barrier islands continues to grow seaward, and lagoons behind these islands continue to fill with sand and clay brought down by rivers.

As seen from the surface, the geologic development presents a simple picture of younger and younger rocks overlapping each other toward the coast. However, the same basic forces have contributed to formation of salt domes and complex fault systems resulting in numerous oil and gas fields in the region.

To the traveller, the most evident change is from forested or brush-covered grazing lands in the north and west through the feed, peanut and watermelon growing belt to rich cotton and rice lands along the coast.

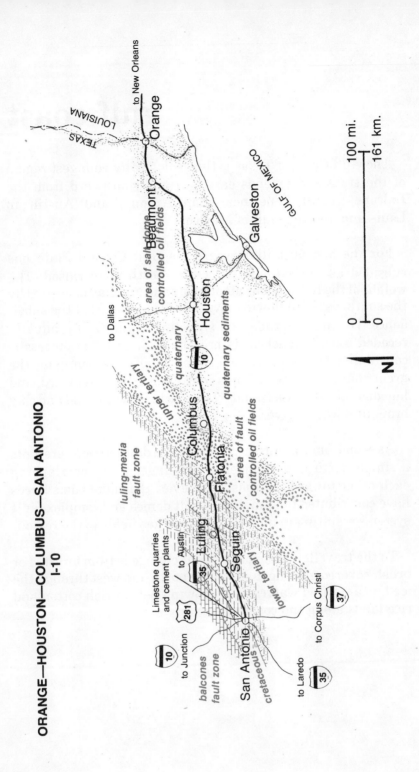

ORANGE—HOUSTON—COLUMBUS—SAN ANTONIO
I-10

interstate 10
orange—houston
—columbus

This stretch of highway offers little of obvious geologic interest. With the exception of Recent muds and sands deposited by rivers within the last 10,000 years, the landscape is a monotonous series of sands and clays deposited in the recent geologic past. The rivers originate hundreds of miles inland and the sediments they have deposited, together with those of their ancestral rivers, helped form the vast coastal plains. It is interesting to realize you are driving over the surface of some 50,000 feet (15,000 meters) of water-lain rocks, and to speculate on the great work waters of the rivers and seas have done to accumulate those rocks.

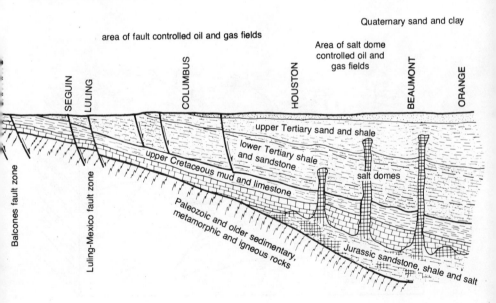

Diagramatic section across the Gulf Coast Basin.

This tremendous mantle of sediments is responsible for two distinct but related phenomena of great importance to the Gulf Coast area. It provides the source—largely in the form of ancient marine life—of great volumes of oil and gas which have to a large degree been responsible for the economic prosperity of the area. The withdrawal of these fluids and of the ground-water is also responsible for minor subsidence of parts of the land surface in the Houston-Galveston region. Lowering of the land surface has reached as much as six feet in the past twenty years. That is minor compared to the total thickness of the rocks, but none-the-less understandably disturbing to those property owners whose homes are near sea level and thus subject to flooding. The responsible mechanism is simple gravity; the oil, gas and water in their liquid forms are essentially incompressible as are the porous sands from which the fluid is produced. However, as fluids are withdrawn from the reservoir rocks, they are replaced by water from the overlying—and underlying—clays and shales. These rocks are then compressed by the weight of the rocks above them, and the land surface subsides with attendant flooding in low coastal areas. Proper control of production practices, particularly from shallow water sands, has effectively reduced the rate of subsidence in the Houston area.

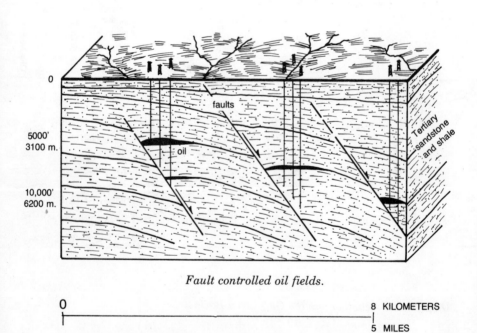

Fault controlled oil fields.

Much of the oil and gas produced from the wells along this part of I-10, comes from salt domes such as those shown on the cross-section and illustrated in more detail by a sketch based on the famous Spindletop field near Beaumont.

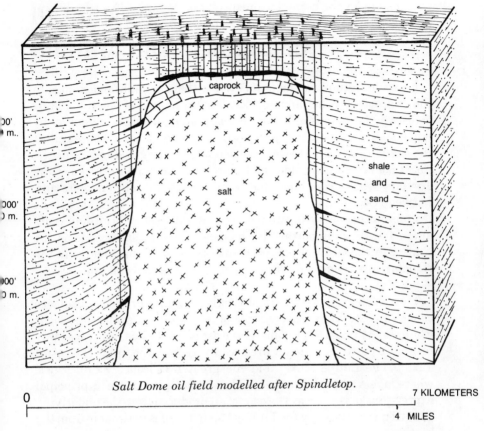

Salt Dome oil field modelled after Spindletop.

The salt that forms the domes was deposited during early Mesozoic time some 200 million years ago when the water of the restricted seas evaporated. As the weight of 50,000 feet (15,000 meters) or so of sediments deposited on top of the salt increased with the passage of many millions of years, the salt behaved as though it were tooth-paste, squeezing upward for thousands of feet. The disruption of layers of rock caused the oil and gas to accumulate to form the oilfields or "pools" from which it is now being withdrawn.

For information on connecting roads, see

Chapter XI
Interstate 10: Columbus—San Antonio

interstate 10
columbus—san antonio

Between Columbus and San Antonio there is a marked change in the character of the land surface. The sameness of Coastal Plains gives way to increasingly varied topography, marked in general by northeast-southwest trending low ridges and valleys. These reflect the transition from the less consolidated young sediments of the Coastal Plains to the older and more erosion-resistant rocks of the Tertiary which were deposited from three to 80 million years ago. Between Seguin and San Antonio, sediments of the later part of the Cretaceous appear. They were deposited from 80 to 100 million years ago. At least as important to the aspect of the countryside as the change in character of the sediments, is the profound change in the structural geologic conditions which have affected the area.

The Coastal region is marked mostly by simple gravity subsidence caused by the increasing weight of accumulated sediments. Near Flatonia, 34 miles (55 kilometers) west of Columbus, this gives way to a more positive, dynamic area resulting from the uplift of Central Texas. The Luling-Mexia and the greater Balcones Fault Zones, where layers of rock have been broken and displaced, are its principal expressions in this area. The odor of oil produced from the underlying Cretaceous rocks along the Luling-Mexia trend is noticeable from the highway

Near San Antonio are large quarries and cement plants where the limestones of the upper Cretaceous are being mined and processed. These rocks have been raised to the surface by the Balcones Fault Zone.

For information on connecting roads, see

Chapter IV
   Interstate 10: San Antonio—Kerrville—Junction
   Interstate 35: Georgetown—Austin—San Antonio
   U.S. 281: San Antonio—Lampasas

SITES OF GEOLOGIC INTEREST

Geothermal Energy: The energy resource of Texas in terms of oil and gas are well known, if sometimes imperfectly understood. A vast potential source of energy exists in the hot waters trapped in the Tertiary sandstones of the Gulf Coast area, where the combination of faulting and salt movement has led to above-normal temperatures and pressures and the accumulation of such higher hydrocarbons as methane.

For several years these accumulations have been studied by state and federal agencies. Water temperatures are in excess of 300 degrees Fahrenheit (150 degrees Celsius), and the gas content is 40 to 50 cubic feet per barrel. A successful geothermal well, which may require a depth of some 15,000 feet should produce hot water at a rate of 20 to 40 thousand barrels per day. Upon reaching the surface, the hot water will convert to steam to power conventional electric generating plants, as is now done in many areas of the world. Such a well would produce well over one million cubic feet of gas per day.

Although the energy potential is enormous, so are the mechanical problems of obtaining it. Nevertheless, this may become an important factor in our future economic picture.

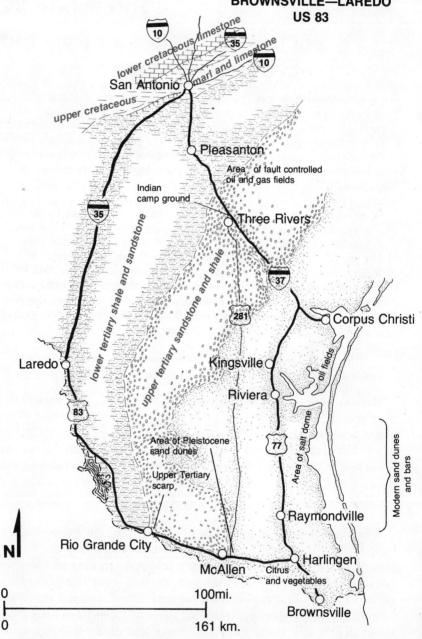

SAN ANTONIO—CORPUS CHRISTI
I-37

CORPUS CHRISTI—BROWNSVILLE
US 77

BROWNSVILLE—LAREDO
US 83

lower cretaceous limestone

marl and limestone

upper cretaceous

San Antonio

Pleasanton

Area of fault controlled
oil and gas fields

Indian
camp ground

lower tertiary shale and sandstone

Three Rivers

upper tertiary sandstone and shale

Corpus Christi

Laredo

Kingsville

Riviera

oil fields

Area of Pleistocene
sand dunes

Area of salt dome

Upper Tertiary
scarp

Modern sand dunes
and bars

Raymondville

N

Rio Grande City

Harlingen

McAllen

Citrus
and vegetables

0	100mi.
0	161 km.

Brownsville

interstate 37
corpus christi—san antonio

Fifteen miles (24 kilometers) from the center of Corpus Christi, I-37 crosses U.S. 77 in sands and clays deposited in Pleistocene time about one million years ago. Many pumping wells, gas processing installations and pipelines attest that this is in the heart of the prolific oil and gas country of the Gulf Coast. Forty-two miles (68 kilometers) from Corpus Christi, I-37 crosses a pronounced ridge of sand and gravel marking the base of the Quaternary and the top of the Tertiary. The view westward from the rest area here is over plains which extend with little interruption to San Antonio. To the southwest is the upper end of Lake Corpus Christi which is a fine example of man's use of natural geologic features. The dam which impounds waters of the Nueces River to form this lake, was built where the basal Pleistocene escarpment provides a natural topographic break in an otherwise almost featureless slope from the Balcones Fault Zone to the sea. The topographic prominence of this ridge is due to the formation of caliche, a limy deposit left at the surface by underground waters that move upward through the porous layers of sand and evaporate.

Midway between Corpus Christi and San Antonio, I-37 crosses the next prominent topographic—and geologic—feature just northwest of the point where U.S. 281 joins I-37. This is the crest of the line of white hills that has been visible for several miles, and marks the lower part of the upper Tertiary. The white color is due to volcanic ash blown out of volcanoes far to the west some 25 million years ago and carried by wind and water currents to the coast line that existed then.

Wherever erosion or road-cuts have cut into and exposed these rocks, a startlingly white contrast to the brown and dirty-grey countryside is apparent. A favorite story told to beginning students of geology in Texas relates that one of the great 19th Century geologists, who first explored on horseback and mapped this then formidable "brush country," recorded these white rocks as limestone. He evidently saw them from a distance and didn't bother to ride through the intervening miles of thorny brush and cactus to investigate.

The topographic prominence of this ridge is in part due to caliche like that described near Corpus Christi, although the rocks here are about twenty million years older. Between deposition of the lower and upper parts of the Tertiary, there was a gap of several million years, and the earliest upper Tertiary rocks laid down were mostly coarse sands deposited where the rivers reached the sea. These are very porous and permit ready circulation of sub-surface water. Where this water reached the surface it evaporated and left the limy rock known as caliche, which is more resistant to erosion than the surrounding sands and clays. A comparison of the two localities gives an excellent example of "uniformitarianism," the basic geologic principle that the physical and chemical processes which we can see at present were responsible for similar results in the distant past.

From this point onward to San Antonio, I-37 crosses older and older Tertiary rocks, until it reaches the Cretaceous rocks at the Balcones Fault Zone.

SITES OF GEOLOGIC INTEREST

Less than one mile southeast of the junction of U.S. 281 and I-37 near Three Rivers, there is a site used by Indians as a camping or temporary staging area from about 8000 years ago until the 15th century. In 1978 this was being investigated by the archeological branch of the Texas Department of Highways in preparation for the completion of I-37.

Excavating ancient Indian campsite near Three Rivers. The rocks are Quaternary sands deposited along the ancestral Atascosa River several thousand years ago.

166

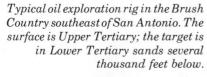

Close view of artifacts and bones embedded in sand. The bones on the pedestal are human.

Uranium-bearing ores are common in the upper Tertiary sandstone and shale in this area. They are extracted from open pits or strip mines, or by underground solution. Both mines and processing plants can be seen from I-37.

Typical oil exploration rig in the Brush Country southeast of San Antonio. The surface is Upper Tertiary; the target is in Lower Tertiary sands several thousand feet below.

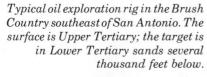

167

The nearly horizontal layering of the upper Tertiary sand and clay is evident in this worked-out pit. Present regulations require that all such areas be restored to their original state.

For information on connecting roads, see

u.s. 77
corpus christi—brownsville

From the northwestern limit of the city of Corpus Christi where it crosses I-37, to the Mexican border at Brownsville, U.S. 77 crosses generally flat terrain. For the first 45 miles (72 kilometers) it is on Pleistocene (lower Quaternary) beach and river deposits laid down about one million years ago. From Riviera to the Mexican border, the surface is even more recent except just north of Raymondville and about sixty miles (97 kilometers) south of I-37 where "fossilized" sand dunes form low rounded hills. These old sand dunes are Pleistocene, and they mark the line of the coast at that time. The same type of sand deposits may be seen today along the beaches and barrier islands of the Gulf Coast. They have been stabilized by the growth of vegetation and by the deposition near the surface of various minerals left by evaporating waters.

There is little surface evidence other than occasional drilling rigs and pumping wells to show that this part of the Gulf Coast is formed of many tens of thousands of feet of sediments. Salt domes, similar to those in the Houston area, trap numerous accumulations of oil and gas.

Between Kingsville and Raymondville, almost all of U.S. 77 is built on the King Ranch which, at over one million acres, ranks as one of the largest private cattle ranches in the world. It was here that the Santa Gertrudis strain of beef cattle was developed by crossing tick- and worm-resistant Brahma stock from South Asia with the heavy meat-producing cross-breed of Herefords and Longhorns to attain the better characteristics of each.

During the earlier decades of the 20th century, the ranch resembled an autonomous kingdom, and travellers were often challenged by armed men on horseback who patrolled the open range.

For information on connecting roads, see

Chapter X
Interstate 27: Corpus Christi-San Antonio U.S. 83: Brownsville-Laredo

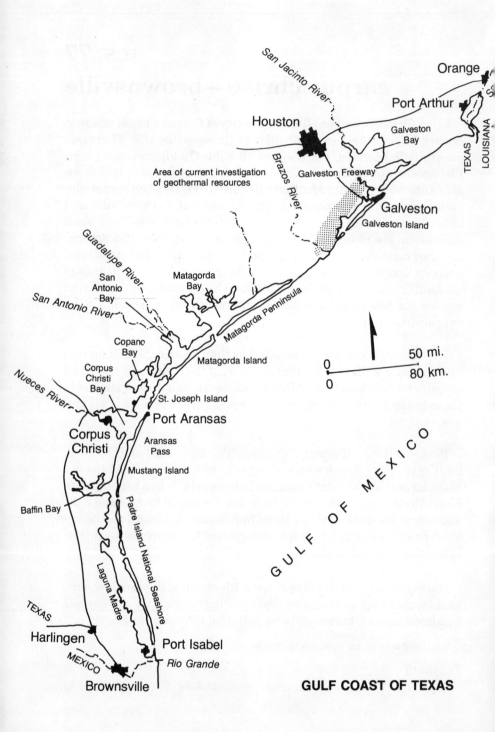

San Jacinto River

Orange

Port Arthur

Houston

Galveston Bay

TEXAS

LOUISIANA

Galveston Freeway

Area of current investigation of geothermal resources

Brazos River

Galveston

Galveston Island

Guadalupe River

Matagorda Bay

San Antonio Bay

San Antonio River

Matagorda Penninsula

Copano Bay

Matagorda Island

Corpus Christi Bay

St. Joseph Island

0   50 mi.

0   80 km.

Nueces River

Port Aransas

Corpus Christi

Aransas Pass

G U L F   O F   M E X I C O

Mustang Island

Baffin Bay

Padre Island National Seashore

Laguna Madre

TEXAS

Harlingen

MEXICO

Port Isabel

Rio Grande

Brownsville

GULF COAST OF TEXAS

170

SITES OF GEOLOGIC INTEREST

Barrier Islands: The shoreline of the Gulf of Mexico, as it may be seen today, offers a beautiful example of the way in which the entire Gulf Coast region of Texas has developed over the past 60 million years or so, or since early Tertiary time.

Broadly speaking, the coast of the Gulf of Mexico is a long smooth arc. It is made irregular only by the estuaries and deltas of the rivers that flow into it to deposit the sands and muds washed down from the higher inland areas. These river-carried sediments reach the sea as muddy waters. They are deposited when the flow of the water is slowed upon reaching the ocean, and are then distributed along the coast by the ocean currents flowing northward from Mexico. Thus the rather ragged arc is smoothed by the chain of barrier islands and peninsulas which extends along the entire Texas coast from Mexico to Louisiana.

The waves of the sea are gentle swells in the open water, but become turbulent surf upon reaching the shore. They churn the sands and muds and winnow out the finer particles to leave the sand-sized fragments, plus innumerable shells, to form the present beaches. The end result is the series of barrier islands which marks the entire coast of Texas.

Where these beach sands are above water level, the winds whip them into dunes or miniature hills, and the islands are formed. Various grasses and other plants whose seeds have been brought in by wind and water currents take root and protect the loose sands from further erosion or transportation.

This interaction of the forces of rivers, waves and winds continues as it has for many millions of years, and may be seen anywhere along the Texas coast. The action is progressive, with the form of the dunes changing visibly from hour to hour.

Here we go back to the principle of "uniformitarianism" which was mentioned in the Corpus Christi—San Antonio part of this book. The same combination of natural forces is responsible for the older sand dunes north of Raymondville and west of Harlingen, and for the much older sands from which oil is produced between the present Gulf Coast and the Balcones Fault Zone. The same principle is valid for rocks of any geologic age.

These photos were taken from the same point; the one on the left in the evening and the one on the right the next morning. They show how the aspect of the shoreline can change over-night. These same processes have been acting over 10's of millions of years along the present and ancestral Gulf Coast.

The easiest way for the traveller to view the barrier islands is by crossing the causway from Aransas Pass to Port Aransas at the northern tip of Mustang Island. From here a paved road follows the landward side of the dunes to another causeway which leads back to Corpus Christi. A better view of the islands and their development may be had by driving eastward from Harlingen or Brownsville to Port Isabel and crossing the bridge to the southern tip of Padre Island. The first few miles northward along Padre Island are well developed and provided with good roads. It is possible to drive the entire length of the island chain from Port Isabel to Corpus Christi, but such a trip requires four-wheel-drive and an intimate knowledge of the tides and weather conditions. It is not recommended for the casual traveller.

u.s. 83
brownsville—laredo

"The Valley" is the lower reaches of the Rio Grande or the Rio Bravo del Norte as the early Spaniards so aptly named it. It is a region of unspectacular geology, which because of its equable year-round climate, supports a unique sub-culture. This is the citrus and vegetable-growing, sub-tropical zone visited each winter by the "Snow-Birds" or "Winter Texans" from the northern states and the Canadian Provinces in search of a respite from their frigid weather. At any restaurant or service station the conversation between the trailer and camper transients is the same. "How was the weather when you left home?" "What rear-axle ratio do you use?" "How much does your trailer parking lot charge?"

From Harlingen toward Laredo, U.S. 83 crosses roughly 50 miles (80 kilometers) of flat, alluvial country-side with citrus groves and often huge vegetable gardens. Near Palm View the scenery changes abruptly as the landscape is broken by sand dunes similar to those north of Raymondville.

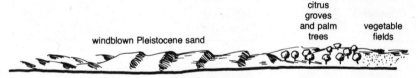

windblown Pleistocene sand

citrus groves and palm trees

vegetable fields

Northwestern end of the "Valley" near Palm View.

This was a Pleistocene shoreline when the coast was farther inland than it is now. It is the end of the fertile alluvial valley with its vegetable fields, citrus groves and ornamental palm trees irrigated by water from the Rio Grande; and is the beginning of the thorny brush-covered cattle land that extends from here to Laredo.

Near Rio Grande City the next big topographic break exposes sandstones of the upper Tertiary which form a west-facing scarp.

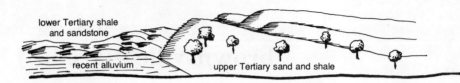

lower Tertiary shale and sandstone

recent alluvium

upper Tertiary sand and shale

Four miles east of Rio Grande City.

From Rio Grande City to Laredo, U.S. 83 stays in lower Tertiary sediments with the shale layers forming valleys and the more resistant sandstones forming low hills. Midway along this stretch of highway, Falcon Lake is visible to the southwest. The lake is a result of a cooperative Mexican-U.S. dam across the Rio Grande, and is a mecca for bass fishermen from both countries.

The hazy mountains that may be seen on the skyline 50 miles (80 kilometers) to the southwest are the northern end of the Sierra Madre Oriental near Monterrey, Mexico.

For information on connecting roads, see

Chapter VIII
    Interstate 35: San Antonio—Laredo
Chapter X
    U.S. 77: Corpus Christi—Brownsville

Glossary

In spite of all efforts to avoid using specialized jargon, a few such words appear in this book. Perhaps this glossary will help the reader.

Algae. Primitive seaweed; one of the first forms of life.

Alluvium. A deposit of sand or mud formed by flowing water.

Anhydrite. Literally, without water. Specifically, a sulfate of calcium deposited when mineral-rich water evaporates. Gypsum without the water.

Arch. An upward bending of rock layers.

Ash. Residue from burning. Geologically, fine particles of crystallised silica from a volcano.

Basalt. A dark colored volcanic rock. The most commonly seen type of lava.

Batholith. A large body of igneous rock that intruded older rocks and solidified far below the Earth's surface.

Calcite. Calcium carbonate. One of the most common rocks and a major constituent of sea shells. Generally deposited by sea-water as limestone.

Cambrian. The oldest geological period of which we have fossil record. The name derives from Cambria or Wales, and it includes the time from some 700 to 500 million years ago.

Carboniferous. Literally, the time of coal. That part of geologic time from 330 to 270 million years ago when tree-like plants were the dominant form of life. The Mississippian and Pennsylvanian periods.

Cenozoic. The geologic era covering the most recent 80 million years and including the Tertiary and Quaternary epochs. From the Greek words meaning common or now-known life.

Chert. A compact sedimentary rock consisting primarily of quartz without evident crystalline form.

Conglomerate. A sedimentary rock composed of gravel or boulder size rock fragments deposited by moving currents of water.

Cretaceous. The geological period extending from about 140 to 80 million years ago. Limestone is the dominant rock type as is implied by the name from the Latin for "chalk."

Crust. The rigid outer part of the Earth generally extending to a depth of about 60 miles (100 km.).

Delta. The muds and sands deposited by a river where it reaches the sea. So-called because of its common roughly triangular shape.

Devonian. The middle part of the Paleozoic Era extending for about 70 million years, from about 400 million years ago. Named for its wide-spread exposure in the Devon area of England.

Dike. A generally narrow and elongate body of igneous rock formed when magma was squeezed into a fracture zone.

Eocene. The period of Tertiary time between about 80 and 40 million years ago. Literally "dawn of recent".

Evaporite. A sedimentary rock composed of minerals such as salt and gypsum which result from the evaporation of salt water.

Extrusive. An igneous rock, such as lava, which formed when magma spread out and cooled on the Earth's surface.

Fault. A fracture in the Earth's crust separating blocks that shifted past each other. Commonly distinguished because the rocks on the either side do not match.

Flint. Similar to chert, but commonly occuring in nodules. Its extreme hardness and flaky fracture made it a favorite for arrow points, axes, etc.

Fossil. Any remains or trace of an animal or plant that lived in the geologic past, as a shell, skeleton, leaf impression or foot-print.

Glacial. Pertaining to or caused by moving ice sheets. Generally used to describe the great continental glaciers that covered much of the Earth's surface during the Pleistocene period from about 3 to 1 million years ago.

Gneiss. A common metamorphic rock composed of re-formed mineral crystals. Somewhat resembles a streaky granite. Pronounced "nice".

Granite. An igneous rock composed of quartz and feldspar with some dark minerals. Generally grey to pink in color.

Gypsum. An evaporite composed of calcium sulfate and water.

Hiatus. A gap in the geologic record; an unconformity.

Hornblende. A shiny black or dark green mineral common in most igneous and metamorphic rocks.

Ice Age. Any time characterized by major glaciers. Generally used for the Pleistocene period.

Igneous. Any rock that has solidified from a molten state. From the Latin for fire.

Inlier. An outcrop of older rocks completely surrounded by younger rocks.

Intrusive. An igneous rock that solidified when the magma crystallized below the surface.

Jurassic. The geologic period from about 180 to 140 million years ago. Named for the Jura Alps in Europe.

Lava. The hardened rock which flowed from a volcano.

Limestone. A sedimentary rock formed largely of calcium carbonate. Commonly contains marine fossils.

Lithology. The science dealing with rocks, and thus the physical and chemical characteristics of rocks.

Magma. Any molten rock.

Marl. An impure limestone or a limy clay.

Mesozoic. The geologic era between the Paleozoic and the Cenezoic and including the Triassic, Jurassic and Cretaceous. It includes the time from about 250 to 80 million years ago. The name means middle life. In older literature it is called "Secondary".

Metamorphic. Changed in form; thus rock whose character has been altered as by heat and pressure.

Mica. A common mineral in igneous and metamorphic rock. It may vary from white to black, but always splits easily into thin flat flakes or booklets.

Mineral. The inorganic crystals or fragments of which rocks are formed.

Miocene. That part of the Tertiary period extending from about 25 to 11 million years ago. Literally "less recent".

Mississippian. The oldest part of the Carboniferous period of the middle Paleozoic. Named from its wide exposure in Mississippi, and in Texas considered as the youngest part of the lower Paleozoic or as the time of transition from lower to upper Paleozoic. About 330 to 300 million years old.

Normal Fault. A fracture in the Earth's crust caused primarily by a pulling apart of the rock due to subsiding caused by gravity.

Oligocene. The middle part of the Tertiary epoch extending from about 40 to 25 million years ago. The name means that few modern life forms were then existent.

Orodovician. The lower Paleozoic period from about 500 to 400 million years ago. Named from an ancient British tribe in northern Wales; a time of widespread limestone-depositing seas in Texas.

Outlier. An erosional remnant of younger rocks perched on older rocks.

Overthrust. A fault or fracture where older rocks are pushed up and over younger rocks. A thrust fault.

Paleozoic. Literally "old life".The time when recognizable forms of life first appeared on Earth from about 600 to 250 million years ago. Sometimes called "Primary".

Pegmatite. A coarse grained form of granite having crystals at least an inch (2.5 cm.) across; almost always occurs as dikes. Often a good place to collect mineral specimens.

Pennsylvanian. The part of the Paleozoic time between the Mississippian and the Permian, or between about 300 and 270 million years ago.

Permian. The youngest period of Paleozoic time, between abut 270 and 250 million years ago.

Pleistocene. The earliest part of Quaternary time from about 3 to 1 million years ago. Often called the Glacial or Ice Age. Literally "near recent".

Pliocene. The youngest part of Tertiary time or about 10 million to 3 million years ago. Literally "more recent".

Precambrian. The interval of time between the age of the oldest known rocks — about 4 billion years — and the start of Cambrian time about 600 million years ago.

Quartz. One of the most common minerals in most rocks, whether igneous or sedimentary. Silicon dioxide.

Quaternary. All time since the Tertiary ended about 3 million years ago.

Radiometric. Referring to the measurement of the changes in elements by the loss of radiant energy. Widely used in estimating the age of rocks.

Recent. The last million years or so of the Earth's history.

Rhyolite. A light colored variety of volcanic rock often including volcanic ash.

Rock. Any naturally occurring, but inorganic, combination of minerals.

Sandstone. A sedimentary rock originally deposited as sand. The individual grains can generally be seen.

Schist. A common metamorphic rock with a streaky or layered appearance caused by the presence of mica.

Sediment. Any natural material that has been transported and deposited by water or wind.

Shale. A very fine grained sedimentary rock deposited in relatively thin layers.

Silica. Silicon dioxide or quartz in its many forms.

Siltstone. A sedimentary rock with grains too coarse to be shale or clay, and too fine to be sandstone.

Silurian. That part of Paleozoic time between the Ordovocian and the Devonian or about 440 to 400 million years ago.

Stock. A small intrusion of igneous rock; often the solidified core of a volcano.

Tectonic. Referring to the forces or conditions within the Earth which cause movements of the crust ranging from minor faults to the building of mountain ranges.

Tertiary. The interval of time between the end of the Cretaceous about 80 million years ago and the beginning of the Quaternary about 3 million years ago.

Thrust Fault. A fracture in the Earth's crust where older rocks have been pushed over younger rocks.

Triassic. The interval of time between the end of the Paleozoic about 250 million years ago and the start of the Jurassic about 180 million years ago.

Unconformity. The contact between two or more well defined sequences of rocks where a significant time interval elapsed. Commonly accompanied by erosion and perhaps tilting of the older rocks before deposition of the younger.

Unconsolidated. Loose sedimentary material not hardened or cemented into solid rock.

Valley Fill. Sedimentary material such as gravel, sand or mud deposited in a valley.

Vein. Any mineral deposit that fills a fracture in older rocks. May be either igneous or sedimentary.

Weathering. The various surface processes that break up or decompose solid rock to form soil.

Selected References

There is a wealth of excellent literature containing information about the geology of Texas, and the very few publications listed here are only those considered to command the widest interest. The Bureau of Economic Geology is the best source of such information, and anyone wanting more detailed descriptions should consult the Bureau's List of Publications. The numerous *Guide Books* and the *Geological Atlas of Texas* are particularly valuable.

American Association of Petroleum Geologists: *Geological Highway Map of Texas* (1973).

Bureau of Economic Geology, University of Texas at Austin: *Energy Resources of Texas*, Ann E. St. Clair et al (1976); *Geology of Big Bend National Park*, Ross Maxwell et al (1967); *Geology of Texas*, Vol. I *Stratigraphy*, E.H. Sellards, W.S. Adkins and F.B. Plummer (1932), Vol. II *Structural and Economic Geology*, E.H. Sellards and C.L. Baker (1934); *Geologic and Historic Guide to the State Parks of Texas*, Ross Maxwell et al (1970); *Land Resources of Texas*, R.S. Kier, L.E. Garner, and L.F. Brown (1977); *Texas Fossils*, W.H. Matthews III (1960).

Texas Memorial Museum: *Texas Through 250,000,000 Years* (1939).

(Those items marked with an asterisk are specifically designed for the non-geologist.)